Essays on Muslims & Multiculturalism

Essays on Muslims & Multiculturalism

Edited by Raimond Gaita

With contributions by

Waleed Aly, Ghassan Hage,
Graeme Davison, Shakira Hussein,
Geoffrey Brahm Levey, Raimond Gaita

TEXT PUBLISHING MELBOURNE AUSTRALIA

The paper in this book is manufactured only from wood grown in sustainable regrowth forests.

The Text Publishing Company
Swann House
22 William Street
Melbourne Victoria 3000
Australia
textpublishing.com.au

First published by The Text Publishing Company, 2011

Cover design by W H Chong
Page design by Susan Miller
Typeset by J & M Typesetting
Printed and bound in Australia by Griffin Press

National Library of Australia
Cataloguing-in-Publication entry

Title: Essays on muslims and multiculturalism / Raimond Gaita (editor).

Edition: 1st ed.

ISBN: 9781921656606 (pbk.)

Subjects: Muslims--Australia.
Multiculturalism--Australia.

Dewey Number: 305.6970994

CONTENTS

INTRODUCTION

Before September 11, 2001, much of the argument in Australia about multiculturalism was a trumped up affair: it had little to do with multiculturalism as it actually functioned here and elsewhere in the world. Confined almost entirely to the intelligentsia, it suffered the deformations that afflict almost everything that attracts the attention of cultural combatants: oversimplification, the proliferation of straw men, false alternatives and rancour, to name only a few.

Until the 1960s Australians demanded that immigrants assimilate to what John Hirst describes as the historically distinctive Antipodean mix of Anglo-Celtic cultures that we call 'Australian'.[1] It was a demand that showed little understanding of the need many immigrants felt to acknowledge and often to celebrate the cultures that shaped their identities. In the late 1960s Australian culture opened to voices that spoke from roots in Europe, Asia, the Middle East and elsewhere—an act of generosity that changed irreversibly almost everyone's understanding of what it means to be Australian. The conversation is ongoing and, as with all real conversation, no one can predict how it will end. That, of course, is unsettling, and Australians have responded differently at different times. Sometimes they welcome it; sometimes it makes them anxious. Most of them accept it most of the time. That is why Australians and foreigners rightly believe that Australia is a highly successful multicultural nation.

When John Howard's government committed Australia to the 'war on terror', it brought argument about multiculturalism into the political mainstream. Howard had always been, at best, ambivalent about multiculturalism. In a speech in 1977 at the Melbourne Town Hall he appeared to give qualified support to it, but he also said that it had already existed since at least the 1940s.[2] Under the guise of praising multiculturalism Howard praised ethnically and religiously tolerant assimilationalism.[3] Did he know what he was doing? I don't know, but in a notorious speech to the

Sydney Institute in 2006, his treasurer, Peter Costello, did much the same. 'Australia is often described as a successful multicultural society [and] it is *in the sense that* people from all different backgrounds live together in harmony,' he said.[4] In that same speech he spoke contemptuously of 'mushy multiculturalism'. I assume that he intended to exploit the ambiguity of a phrase that enabled him either to characterise only some forms of multiculturalism as mushy or to characterise all forms of it as that.[5]

If one abstracts many of the things that Howard, Costello and others said about the responsibilities and privileges of citizenship from the tone in which they said them, then they sound like platitudes. 'Loyalty, democracy, tolerance, the rule of law: values worth promoting, values worth defending',[6] Costello proclaimed. He was right, of course: citizenship is a great good. Anyone who values it and who acknowledges the serious responsibilities it imposes on those who benefit from it will try to ensure that the conditions for its enjoyment are not eroded. But the tone in which Costello and others expressed those and other sentiments was aggressively populist and jingoistic, and nobody doubted that it was directed at Muslims: 'Before entering a mosque visitors are asked to take off their shoes. This is a sign of respect. If you have a strong objection to walking in your socks don't enter the mosque. Before becoming an Australian you will be asked to subscribe to certain values. If you have strong objections to those values don't come to Australia.'[7]

The aftermath of September 11 was not a time when political judgment flourished. In order to be just to the Howard government and the governments of other nations, we must remember how hard it was to keep one's bearings, morally and politically. Many people whose judgment had hitherto generally been sensible spoke as though something radically new and alien had entered the political world. A British journalist said that strange, and perhaps offensive, though it may at first seem, the suicide bombers in the Middle East acknowledge limits to what they may justifiably do. The terrorists who flew the hijacked planes with their passengers into the towers respected no limits, he went on to say. In the ruins of the towers, many saw the spectre of an essentially apolitical nihilism that would stalk the earth, uninhibited by an unspoken consensus about the nature of political activity that set limits to even radical, brutal or tyrannical politics. Perhaps that is why reality could not constrain the rhetoric of our political leaders. As much as they exploited the confusion with varying mixtures of cynicism and opportunism, politicians were themselves victims of an intoxicating mixture of horror, dread and excitement.

To be just, we must also ask, 'Compared to what?' as Martin Krygier has repeatedly urged us to when we are morally critical of the political conduct of a nation, especially our own[8]. Australia was less damaged by the 'war on terror' than was Britain where it fed the sanctimonious authoritarianism instinctive to Tony Blair and Gordon Brown and was therefore used to license assaults on liberties. In many European nations jingoistic nationalism was and continues to be more virulent and dangerous than it is in Australia. To protect her party against the xenophobic right, even the German Chancellor, Angela Merkel, felt compelled to declare multiculturalism dead in Germany.

Nonetheless, Australians have no reason to be complacent. There is at least a case for saying that the threat of terrorism awakened in many Europeans anxieties about nationhood and multiculturalism that had existed for many years before September 11. Australians can make no such claim. In Australia, before September 11, for the most part, only cultural combatants doubted the success and value of Australian multiculturalism. Many Australians were proud of it and foreigners admired it. Howard, Costello and others who attacked it after September 11, were not before then hostile to the multicultural reality on the ground. None of them, as far as I know, suggested that we return to the assimilationist practices of the 1950s. When, in the lecture to which I referred earlier, Howard refused to fully acknowledge multiculturalism, but praised instead a racially and ethnically tolerant society, he was not driven by hostility to what he saw on the ground: One of the most ideological of Australian prime minsters, an avid reader of *Quadrant*, which published much of Australian writing hostile to multiculturalism, he was driven by his instinct for cultural combat. In Australia, September 11 did not, as it did in Europe, trigger hitherto suppressed anxieties about immigrants and multiculturalism. It provoked fear of Muslims and, as a natural consequence, groundless hostility to them. Insofar as it focused on multiculturalism, the political argument in Australia after September 11 was trumped up, just as the argument between cultural combatants had been.

Politicians have been mistaken, I believe, to offer opinions on what is true and what is false Islam in the hope of assuaging anxieties that inflammatory talk of the clash of civilisations awakened in many Muslims. The politicians probably had mixed motives, but I'm sure they were, on the whole, well intentioned and sincere. Indeed, generally they said no more than what has become pretty much orthodoxy in the liberal, democratic West, namely, that true religion is humane and tolerant. That orthodoxy prevailed, I suspect, not as the provisional result of scholarly, theological and philosophical debate, but as something many people believe *must* be true.

That may be changing. Many people are now struck by the fact, or perhaps, are struck by the significance of the fact, that there are too many biblical texts and too many theological utterances in support of those whom we call fanatics. We call them fanatics because we assume that they are in the grip of pathological dispositions that cause them radically to corrupt what is respect-worthy in religion. 'True believers' we call them, but the pejorative irony of that expression may owe more to an urbane liberal distaste for intensity than to theological or psychological acumen. Be that as it may: secular liberals have been disinclined to accept that the reasons that 'true believers' (fanatics, fundamentalists) offer to defend their beliefs are the reasons they hold them. That enabled us to find comfort in the belief that were we to ameliorate the social and political misery of peoples in the underdeveloped world, we would undermine the forces that generate the pathologies that make 'true believers' of increasing numbers of them. We should, however, take more seriously the likelihood that radical Muslims of the kind Christopher Hitchens calls Islamofascists are motivated by the reasons they declare and that those reasons are inseparable from their interpretations of religious texts—interpretations that most people are in no position to dispute seriously.

The Australian theologian Tony Kelly once quipped that one could have too much of religion but never too much of God. It is a point to which even atheists might respond sympathetically in order to distinguish belief in the god that they disdain from belief in the god that they respect, even if grudgingly. But leaving mysticism aside, when Christians, Jews and Muslims try reflectively to distinguish the god they believe to be the true god from false gods, how can they do it other than by appeal to their sacred texts? How, for that matter, will they distinguish the true god from the devil who surely has what it takes to put on an imitation of the true god that would be convincing to any ordinary mortal?

In the sacred texts that are common to Jews and Christians, God commands enough massacres of the enemies of the one true God to make anyone's hair stand on end. Can the god who ordered the massacre of women and children and even the animals in Jericho, who spared only a handful of quislings, be the same god who is worshipped in the psalms or who appeared to Job out of the whirlwind? It's an old question, of course, but it now presses urgently and, for some, painfully. A morally identical question can be asked of passages in the Koran. But just as politicians wisely do not comment on the moral questions that biblical texts throw up for serious Christians and Jews, so they should avoid comment on what counts as the right interpretation of the Koran, even when the desire to prevent social strife tempts them to say that terrorists must be motivated by false religion. Although most Muslims acknowledge that the efforts of these politicians on their behalf are well intentioned, many find them presumptuous and condescending. The perception that politicians need to make such efforts on behalf of Muslims but not on behalf of Jews and Christians is dangerous for Muslims.

Like many nations, Australia still has reason to fear potentially devastating terrorist attacks from radicalised Muslims. Everyone acknowledges that the number of 'home-grown' radicals who might commit such attacks on Australians is small and that the majority of Australian Muslims pose no threat to the lives of their fellow citizens, to Australian national identity and values, or to multiculturalism. Despite their connection to fellow jihadists abroad, the Muslims in Australia who might pose a threat to the lives of Australians are essentially a problem for the police, albeit for police in need of support from intelligence organisations at home and abroad. The rhetoric of the war on terror, however, made it seem as though they were a national security problem, or at least a political problem insofar as they could justifiably be portrayed as a threat to civil society in a way that even criminal gangs are not.

Terrorism is not always a threat to civil society even if it always hopes to be. In an article in the *Guardian*, David Grossman describes what it can be like when it is such a threat, as it was when Israel suffered repeated attacks from suicide bombers.

Just a few weeks of life in the shadow of terror will show every nation that believes itself enlightened just how rapidly and sharply it can turn needs into values, let fear determine its norms. Terror humiliates. It rapidly returns a human being into a pre-cultural, violent and chaotic existence. It determines where society's breaking point is. It entices certain groups, not only small ones, to join it, and to actively seek to use force to destroy and crush everything they hate. Terror contains something that acts like a decomposition enzyme—the decomposition of the private human body and the public body...A country that fights terror fights not only for the physical security of its citizens. It also fights for their reason to live, for their humanity, for everything that makes them human and civilised.[9]

Nothing like that could be said of Australia, now or in the foreseeable future. Insofar as a decomposition enzyme has attacked civil society here and in Britain, it was developed and set loose by the governments of those countries. Henry Porter, a journalist for the *Observer*, has written many reports, distressing to anyone who loves Britain, on the attacks on liberty there.[10]

Immediately after the first London bombings in July 2007, then attorney general Philip Ruddock told a meeting of the American Australian Association in New York that he was examining his obligations under Article 3 of the

Universal Declaration of Human Rights. It states, 'Everyone has a right to life, liberty and security of person.' He did not want, he explained, to be the attorney general against whom grieving relatives could complain that he had not done all that he could to protect the lives of Australian citizens.[11]

At around the same time Ruddock said in a radio interview that if there is an absolute right, then it is the right to life. That sounds impressive, but no politician can believe it. All political leaders will, when necessary, conscript their citizens and send them to war, not usually in order to protect the conditions under which they can live safely, but to protect distinctively political ideals and needs.

The obligation on governments to protect the lives of their citizens is, of course, a serious one, but it can be overridden when, for example, the only available means to protect lives undermine institutions that enable us to live with honour and decency as a body politic. In such circumstances we can think that for moral reasons we should renounce the means available to protect ourselves though it will be at some cost to the common good, or we can think that it should be part of our conception of the common good that we do not even contemplate using such means. The second is a deeper conception of the common good and therefore of the national interest.

Terrorists threaten only our lives. They do not threaten the values that we hold dear. We do that if, to save our lives, we seriously degrade institutions that we cherish—the very institutions that an aggressor would destroy if he were to occupy us.

Ruddock wanted to let civil libertarians know that two can play the human rights game. At the crunch, he was telling them, the protection of life trumps the protection of liberty. But that, I am sure, was not his only purpose. Ruddock oversaw with chilling efficiency the incarceration, behind razor wire, of asylum seekers, sometimes with their children and sometimes for years. Ruthless though the policy was, when he defended it he did not find it necessary to play the right-to-life-and-security card. It's a big card to play. Given his and his government's record, Australians had reason to be anxious about what he believed the stakes were. Almost certainly he had in mind how he could defend further changes in the conditions under which people could be detained and what could be done to them when they were. A few days after his new-found respect for his obligations under international law, Ruddock was in discussion with the US attorney-general Alberto Gonzales, the man who called the Geneva Convention a 'quaint document' and who helped to redefine torture in US law so as to exclude from that definition many of the acts that international law counts as falling under it. Courtesy of Tony Abbott, Philip Ruddock has returned to the Coalition front bench.

Long before September 11, many people felt that in the future politics would be dominated by crises caused and inflamed by the shameful gap between the rich and the poor nations, aggravated by the effects of climate change. The urgent questions centred on international human rights, ecological issues and equality between nations as much as equality within them. Today, many people believe that the distinction between what we have an obligation to do as a sovereign nation and what we might freely do for 'humanitarian' reasons (about refugees or asylum seekers, for example) cannot survive much longer in its present form. Actions and policies that we now regard as humane but optional will become political obligations that fall upon us by virtue of our place in the community of nations. The question will be: Why, merely because we are fortunate to be born in a particular location on this earth, should we enjoy wealth, health and security and be able, in the name of sovereignty, to deny it to others who, merely because they are born elsewhere, suffer the miseries and the humiliations of the damned?

That question will become morally unavoidable, especially as Western nations realise, in the bones of their political culture, to what extent their troubles are the result of their colonial adventures. No one, of course, can sensibly believe that anyone should be permitted to live wherever they wish. Who will deny that a nation has the right to deport non-citizens who are serious law breakers or who repeatedly preach hatred of the values that define the political identity of its citizens and for which they are prepared to sacrifice their lives? But if we rise to the question's simple moral force, we will, I hope, rethink the relative importance we attach to an appeal to rights, on the one hand, and to our obligation to need, on the other. In many poor nations the wealthy live behind electrified razor wire. One doesn't have to be a futurologist to foresee their doom, though it remains to be seen whether those who ensure their downfall will take their place behind the wire. Increasingly the defensive policies of the wealthy nations look like national versions of living behind razor wire. They try to justify, as the Howard government and now the Gillard government tried to justify, their mean-spirited response to the needs of asylum seekers by appeal to the rights of sovereign nations. In this context, talk of rights seems very thin and inevitably raises the question: On what are these rights based, what is their justification and what is their extent? If they are placed in the context of the more basic question I raised above, then these questions have the potential to stimulate radical answers.

But this is not a book of high theory. It does not discuss the nature of the state or whether the nation-state is a defunct notion. It offers no systematic answer to how, more seriously and deeply, we can discuss the nature of sovereignty and its limits. I am certain, however, that we cannot, if we desire to be morally and politically sober, speak about Muslims and multiculturalism in the same tone as we are used to in our discussions about what we can justifiably demand of immigrants. We need to understand why immigrants who suffered the many injurious consequences of the colonial exploitation of their countries look incredulous when we lecture them about Western values. To acknowledge that and to urge its acknowledgment in support of multiculturalism is not to yield to cultural relativism. It is only to acknowledge with appropriate humility that we (the citizens of Western nations) often understandably look like hypocrites, that we have been selective in the peoples to whom we applied those values and that sometimes we did not even see the victims of colonial exploitation as fully human and therefore as fit be treated in accord with those values.

The response to Muslims after September 11 would not have been the same if most Muslims were white. Fear of them tapped into a strain of Australian racism that runs deep. It showed itself many times and in many ways during the Howard years. When in August 2001 Howard claimed that asylum seekers had thrown their children from ships into the sea in order to secure their entry into Australia, he is reported to have said, 'I don't want people like that in Australia. Genuine refugees don't do that…they hang on to their children.'[12] Who are 'people like that'? The answer is not people who are prepared to throw their children into the sea in order to secure for themselves the benefits of refugee status in Australia. Taken only at face value the phrase 'people like that' appears to pick out a group by reference to a moral failing that its members share. But the context and tone in which Howard used it ensured that it referred, indeterminately and perhaps not entirely consciously, to people who are believed to be unable to feel about their children as we do about ours, for whom the birth and death of children cannot go deep as it does with 'us'. *Nothing*, indeed, goes deep with 'them' as it does with 'us'. That is what makes them 'them', and the fact that we are not like them, makes us 'us'.

In Australia, though not in Europe, discussion of multiculturalism has gone into hibernation. It has, however, definitely not yet been resolved. Just as the question of underlying Australian racism has been sharply raised recently by the attacks on Indian students in Melbourne, just as the question of Australian attitudes to asylum has again erupted in ways that shamed the nation and our political leaders, it seems certain that, following the almost inevitable next major terror incident in the West, the heated discussion of Muslims and multiculturalism will return, and, I fear, with a vengeance. This period of relative calm provides an opportunity for reflection on the future health of the great Australian experiment in multicultural migration. To serve such reflection, I offer the reader six essays.

Thanks to Michael Heyward for his patient generosity, and to Jane Pearson for her fine editing.

Raimond Gaita
London, January 2011.

MULTICULTURALISM AND TERROR

Geoffrey Brahm Levey

GEOFFREY BRAHM LEVEY
teaches political theory at the University of New South Wales, Sydney, where he was founding Director of the Program in Jewish Studies. He is editor of *Political Theory and Australian Multiculturalism*, and coeditor (with Tariq Modood) of *Secularism, Religion and Multicultural Citizenship*, and (with Philip Mendes) of *Jews and Australian Politics*.

Multiculturalism as a political theory and public policy has always had its critics. Never before, however, has it faced the chorus of opposition that it does today. Calls for its abolition, if not triumphant pronouncements of its demise, are heard every week. In early 2007, the Howard government erased the term from the federal government's lexicon. The Rudd government retained the purge at the ministerial level, while reinstating 'multicultural' to the title of the parliamentary secretary assisting the minister for immigration and citizenship. The Gillard government has expunged even this remnant of 'multicultural affairs'.[1] It is hard to believe that less than a decade ago multiculturalism looked to be secure and to have won the day.

The changed climate of opinion has been largely prompted by significant Muslim immigration to the West in the post-war period, especially in Europe, the nature of Islam as a 'public religion', and the concomitant rise of global terror, especially its association with Islam and Muslims. But what precisely is the connection between multiculturalism and global terrorism? Does multiculturalism have a case to answer here? In my remarks, I will suggest that while these questions are simple, the answers are complex. Part of the problem with the public debate over multiculturalism and global terror is the assumption that simple questions must have simple answers.

There *is* a global terrorism problem, and it is foolish to deny its association with certain quarters in Islam. But despite the media's quick equations, the role of multiculturalism in this is anything but clear. One can point to a number of more obvious factors behind global terrorism. Among these are surely the protracted Israel–Palestine conflict and, more importantly, the broader historical and cultural currents—of modernisation and colonialism—in which Muslim communities and Western democracies view themselves as well as each other. But there are also contingent factors at work, which are too quickly blamed on multiculturalism.

Writing in 2005 after the London bombings, Terry Lane argued 'assimilation is a sweet word', while multiculturalism is 'a repulsive word denoting an ugly concept'. When I first read this, I thought that Islamists must be seeking to bomb ugly multiculturalism out of existence. In fact, Lane's argument was commonplace: multiculturalism breeds 'ghettos of perpetual difference and special preferment', which are 'bound to foster violence by those who feel either superior to or excluded from the national culture'.[2] For evidence, Lane cited Shehzad Tanweer, one of the British-born, London suicide bombers, whose parents, he says, fled stricken and squalid conditions to come to Britain and a better life, but obviously neglected to assimilate and identify with Britain and British values.

Subsequently, journalists tracked down Tanweer's extended family in Pakistan, who provided some insight into what may have been running through the bomber's mind. 'He knew that excesses are being done to Muslims. Incidents like desecration of the Koran have always been in his mind,' reported his uncle (whom Tanweer had visited in 2004), mentioning specifically the abuse of Muslim prisoners and the desecration of the Koran by US guards at Gauntanamo Bay.[3] Here, then, is a bomber who seems to have been radicalised not by Islamic creed or multicultural pampering or moral relativism or ghettos in Britain, but by the careless reaction to previous Islamic provocations.

So, in looking at multiculturalism, it is important to remember that there's a range of factors, variously deep and contingent, behind episodes of global terrorism, which have little to do with multiculturalism.

Certainly, we should dispatch one contention immediately. The notion that Osama bin Laden and al-Qaeda, and other *jihadi* groups in the Middle East, are the products of Western multicultural policies is simply fanciful. That hasn't, of course, stopped some commentators from claiming this. Nevertheless, the idea is self-evidently absurd, and I don't propose to consider it further.

I shall try instead to disentangle some issues, central to the question, that are usually run together. My argument is that multiculturalism, as we know it, is a way of integrating a culturally diverse population based on shared liberal democratic values. Insofar as multiculturalism is connected to global terrorism at all, it is, I think, not so much because of multiculturalism's commitments as the failure to honour them and their underlying liberal democratic values. I stress that nothing I say in what follows should be construed as justifying or excusing the resort to terror or violence, which I condemn.

What then is the alleged link between multiculturalism and the promotion of terror and civil strife? If one relies on public commentators and editorials, as well as a spate of books—such as Bruce Bawer's *While Europe Slept*, and Melanie Phillip's *Londonistan*[4]—then the 'multicultural syndrome' goes something like this. Western democracies have failed to stand up for their own core values and institutions. They try, in the name of multiculturalism, to be hospitable to all values and cultures, even those inimical to their own. As Janet Albrechtsen put it in a column endorsing Phillip's book, the West is being undone by 'the two commandments of multiculturalism'. One commandment forbids talk that applauds the majority culture. The other forbids criticising minorities.[5] The reference here to 'majority culture' includes both liberal democratic principles and the stuff of national identity, whether British, Dutch, or Australian, etc. The result of this syndrome is said to be a dangerous cocktail of cultural and moral relativism, in which individuals and groups are no longer assimilated to the governing norms of society. This in turn, say the anti-multiculturalists, has spawned the appearance of poisonous doctrines and hostile groups, while enticing Western authorities to leave them unchecked—and to their own, explosive devices. In short, the alleged problem is a kind of variation on Robert Frost's old quip about liberals not being able to take their own side in an argument. Only now liberals are accused of having been encouraged in this spinelessness by their embrace of multiculturalism.

There are three quite distinct claims or assumptions run together in this syndrome, which need to be disentangled. First, and most radically, there is an assumption that Islam and Muslims are fundamentally opposed to Western values. Second, there is the argument that multiculturalism, as a set of principles and policies, sanctions cultural and moral relativism. Third, there is the softer but more comprehensive claim that whatever its stated principles, multiculturalism has, as a matter of general atmosphere or *Zeitgeist*, encouraged these nefarious developments on the ground. Let me address each of these claims in turn.

'Muslims are Unassimilable'

The most radical—and, if true, troubling—claim is that Islam and Muslims are simply locked into a clash of civilisations with the West, to use Samuel Huntington's terminology.[6] On this view, our immigration policies are at fault for importing a hostile and unassimilable alien presence. Indeed, we are committing *politicide* by inviting in a fifth column.

There is an immediate problem with this thesis, which critics of multiculturalism and of Muslims typically downplay. Soon after the London bombings in July 2005, former treasury secretary John Stone, for example, cited a *YouGov* poll that found 6 per cent of Britain's Muslims thought the bombings justified.[7] A former treasury secretary should know that's 94 per cent of British Muslims who *didn't* condone the bombings. Stone also cited findings that sixty Muslims in Australia had training in terrorist activities. That's 0.018 per cent of the 330,000 self-declared Muslims in Australia, a number which Stone himself acknowledges underestimates the number of Muslims here. In other words, at least 99.98 per cent of Australian Muslims have had no truck with terrorist training.

The overwhelming majority of Muslims living in the West seek to integrate and are good, law-abiding citizens. Clearly there are some points of cultural friction, from gender equality to free speech. And a small minority of militant Muslims does agitate violently, in word and deed, against their host societies. The saying, 'All Muslims are not terrorists, but all terrorists are Muslims', is an exaggeration. But it is a fair question to ask why 6 per cent of British Muslims, say, might be disposed to support terror; and perhaps why many more Muslims in Western democracies may be alienated or radicalised, albeit short of resorting to terror.

Here, we need to step back and engage some history. Muslims were not party to the liberal settlements establishing the modern secular state. Nor were they asked, like the Jews, to modernise their religion and traditions and agree to the terms of the newly liberalising nation-states of Europe. Rather, the large Muslim populations in western Europe today are chiefly a product of post-World War II immigration. It needs to be remembered that liberal institutions—limited government, individual rights, rule of law and church-state separation—were forged against the backdrop of protracted and bloody sectarian conflict in early modern Europe. When people say that Muslims refuse to abide by Western practices they forget that the Western practices were devised to reach a political accommodation between the contending religious groups. With the arrival of large numbers of Muslims in the West in recent years, we are witnessing pressures towards a renegotiation of the original liberal settlements.[8] Does this mean abandoning liberal democracy as we know it and starting from scratch? I don't believe so. But it does, I think, mean reviewing how we have gone about practising our principles. It means seeing where our traditional interpretations might be made more accommodating, as well as where cultural minorities must necessarily give ground.

Consider, for a moment, the controversial case of free speech. Cases like the Rushdie affair, the murder of film-maker Theo Van Gogh and the reaction to the Muhammad cartoons in the Danish press are cited as evidence of the basic incompatibility between Muslims and Western norms. There is no doubt that many Muslims do feel that the lampooning or mocking of Islam warrants violent censure, even death. Yet, as British political theorist Bhikhu Parekh notes, there is, in fact, wide disagreement on the issue, with many Muslims disapproving of such censure. The violence aside, the quest to stifle free expression in favour of religious sensibility is also said to be contrary to 'our values'. This loads the issue, however. As Parekh points out, 'Muslims do not question the value of free speech, but its scope and limits.'[9] Many of our long-established religious groups also wish to draw the limits on free speech narrowly rather than broadly, as, indeed, do some liberals. We now have various vilification protocols that make certain kinds of speech about religion and religious groups unlawful. Arguments about the limits of free speech are part of the stuff of free speech. Parekh is right in saying that Muslim protests need not cause undue anxiety as long as they stay within the limits of the law. It follows that where such protests breach the law, they should be answerable to the law.

Moral and Cultural Relativism

Let me turn now to the second claim: that multiculturalism sanctions moral and cultural relativism and thus the idea that anything goes. In his book *Identity and Violence*, economist and Nobel Prize laureate Amartya Sen argued that the very concept of multiculturalism presupposes agreement around a common set of political values.[10] Hence, it opposes moral relativism and cultural separatism. I think this way of putting the matter is a little too neat (as befits, perhaps, an economist). There are, in fact, many different versions of multiculturalism, both in theory and in practice. Multiculturalism is not a single model, just as democracy comes in various formulations: for example, representative, participatory, elitist, statist, and people's democracy—as the Soviet Union and China used to like to call themselves.

What is amazing about the public debate in Australia is how commentators target every version of multiculturalism except the one that we have. In the wake of the 2005 London bombings, conservative commentators (such as Albrechtsen, Andrew Bolt, and Piers Akerman) and some liberal left commentators (such as Terry Lane and the late Pamela Bone) jumped on the 'multiculturalism produces bombers' bandwagon then riding through the British press. In such a derivative culture as Australia's, where so many of our local television programs, for example, are copies of American and British ones, the inclination to assume transcontinental applicability is doubtless hard to resist. But even if requiring some evidence that British multiculturalism was complicit in the London bombings may be asking too much of British commentators, it surely behooves the serious among our own stable to grapple with the policy that applies in Australia.

Writing on the Cronulla riots, Keith Windschuttle advanced the familiar charge that multiculturalism is 'at odds with the core tenets of liberal democracy, where rights inhere in the individual, not the collective'.[11] Most liberal models of multiculturalism are liberal, however, precisely because they *reject* recognising rights for groups as groups. Certainly, Australian multiculturalism, in its various provisions, recognises only the rights of individual Australians to culture and social equity, never group rights.[12] And even here the policy insists on a host of liberal democratic limits. In 2006, then treasurer Peter Costello suddenly denounced what he called 'mushy, misguided multiculturalism'.[13] Anyone would think his own government had not actioned policy statements over the past ten years clearly setting out what Australian multiculturalism is, what it accepts and does not accept. It is very easy to set multiculturalism up as a straw target given the range of versions and meanings available. It is much harder to explain how liberal models like our own violate, rather than more fully realise, liberal principles of autonomy, equality and justice.

There are four basic models of how liberal democracies have sought to respond to cultural diversity. The first is by trying to exclude cultural diversity from entering in the first place. The White Australia Policy is among the best examples of this exclusion. Still, there are only a handful of countries in the world that are even close to being culturally homogeneous. For the rest, cultural diversity has long been a fact of life.

The second model is assimilationism. It has featured in almost every modern nation-state. Indeed, the term 'nation-state' presupposes this idea. That is, not the idea that 'for every nation, its own state'—which is a common formulation of self-determination—but the quite different idea that 'for every state, *one nation*'. (Sounds a tad familiar, doesn't it?) Australia and the other Anglo-democracies fervently pursued this approach until the last third of the twentieth century. They ditched it when it became clear it wasn't working. The liberal expectancy that ethnic groups would assimilate and disappear after a few generations did not eventuate. As the US researchers Glazer and Moynihan famously put it in the 1960s, 'The point about the melting pot is that it did not happen.'[14] State and social pressure on migrants to abandon their mother tongue and cultural heritage more often than not created resentment and social problems. Estrangement saw many migrants return to their home countries. Those who clamour today for a return to assimilation policy need reminding that it was precisely because assimilationism failed that immigrant countries, like Australia, sought alternatives in the first place.

The third model is liberal pluralism, although it goes by various names. On this model, people are allowed to follow their traditions under their own steam, as it were, unassisted by government. Because this model turns largely on the distinction between public and private spheres, all liberal democracies, to some extent, have evidenced it, even when committed to assimilationism. France still very much bridges the assimilationist and liberal pluralist models. While allowing private association and differences, it places enormous stress on the importance of conformity to a common ethos in public arenas. Again, those who recommend assimilationism or a forced acceptance of national values as the answer to hostile minorities should take a close look at the riots and general situation in France in recent years.[15]

Officially, the USA exemplifies the liberal pluralist model. An institution like SBS, for example, is unthinkable in the USA. However, US public law and policy make extensive allowance for cultural diversity, which *in practice* makes the US more like the fourth model: multiculturalism. Here, as we know from the Australian case, government not only allows people to express their cultural attachments, it seeks in law and policy to accommodate, support, and even celebrate such differences.

Liberal democracy is about treating people first and foremost as individuals. Liberal multiculturalism aims to do the same, albeit taking into account their cultural commitments and attachments. In the same way that traditional liberalism mandated the free exercise of religion, within liberal limits, liberal multiculturalism mandates the free exercise of culture, within liberal limits. So, for example, an observant Muslim woman can now wear a specially made veil and join the Victorian Police Force.[16] Who can deny that this better serves liberty, equality, and integration than requiring everyone to wear the identical uniform, or else not do such work? By the same token, cultural practices that infringe on rights and liberties, such as female genital mutilation or the denial of a general education, are rightly disallowed. Liberal multiculturalism, then, is the very opposite of moral and cultural relativism.

Multiculturalism and the *Zeitgeist*

Now, even if the philosophy and policies of liberal multiculturalism do not contradict Western values, one might argue that they nevertheless have had a deleterious impact on Western values. This brings me to the third claim typically linking multiculturalism to terror: namely, that it has encouraged an atmosphere of tolerating the intolerable. Or, as Albrechtsen's 'second commandment' has it, of never daring to criticise minorities. I do not discount this suggestion. I daresay that our multicultural age probably has encouraged some laxity towards certain practices and activities out of mistaken sensitivity to being labelled a bigot, or such like. A certain climate of licence, as against liberty, does seem to have been allowed to take hold in places like Britain and the Netherlands. The obvious answer to such lapses and laxity, however, is a *tightening* adherence to liberal multicultural limits, not the letting go of them.

The failure-to-stand-up-for-our-core-values chorus gets most of the airplay in these discussions. Too little attention is given to what is, I think, a much more potent way in which a failure to abide by our principles helps to undermine integration and promote alienation and violence among minority groups in our community. This is when we proclaim that we are committed to multiculturalism within given limits, but fail to live up to even this much in practice. Or we say we are committed to toleration, and then do not extend it. Or our political leaders demand that Muslims and other minorities respect our democratic values, and then shamelessly flout them themselves.

Asking everyone to play by the rules is fine, in principle. However, it is unlikely to register and bring the desired results of social harmony in the face of entrenched hypocrisy. Until 1998 in Britain, for example, Muslim schools were denied state funding even though they had long been granted to Church of England, Methodist, Catholic, and Jewish schools. In Australia, qualified acceptance is routine among our establishment leaders when they address ethnic minorities, all the while believing that they are being nice and welcoming. I can't recall the number of occasions where assorted dignitaries have addressed the Jewish community by affirming Jews' place in Australian society only after noting the contribution of prominent Jewish figures in business, the professions, the arts, and so on. Apparently, even for an old Australian minority like the Jews—who have resided here ever since ten or so arrived with the First Fleet—being a born or naturalised Australian and a regular law-abiding citizen are not warrant enough to be a valued and equal member of the society.

Contrast this prevailing Australian attitude with the

situation in the USA. When President George Washington addressed the Jews of Newport in 1790, he did not presume to link their acceptance to conspicuous achievement. On the contrary, he stated:

> All possess alike liberty of conscience and immunities of citizenship. It is now no more that toleration is spoken of, as if it was by the indulgence of one class of people that another enjoyed the exercise of their inherent natural rights. For happily the Government of the United States, which gives to bigotry no sanction, to persecution no assistance, requires only that they who live under its protection, should demean themselves as good citizens.[17]

While the USA has, of course, its own history of racism and cultural exclusion, no mainstream US leader today would think to speak to immigrant groups in the USA as if they were anything but equals among Americans. Nor would any Australian leader dream of suggesting that acceptance of Aussie battlers as full Australians is conditional on their making an extraordinary contribution to Australian life.

The hypocrisy reveals itself in other ways. Take Keith Windschuttle's triumphalist 'I told you so' intervention on the Cronulla riots, which rehearsed some all-too-common misapprehensions.[18] For Windschuttle, the riots reflected a cultural and not a racist problem in the Australian community, one for which he blamed our national policy of multiculturalism. For evidence, he pointed to two social facts: the persistence of residential ethnic enclaves, and a trend not to intermarry on the part of Lebanese Muslims in Australia.

Ethnic enclaves are a feature of immigrant patterns historically the world over. They predate the advent of multiculturalism by centuries. Windschuttle himself cites troublesome ethnic enclaves in France and the USA, two countries that do not subscribe to multicultural policy. Indeed, as I noted above, France has long sought to exclude even informal cultural pluralism in the name of an integrated secular republic of like individuals. Yet it has witnessed ethnic-related rioting far more extensive and violent than anything seen in Australia.

That migrants should settle in the same neighbourhoods is, of course, entirely natural. Their kinsfolk who preceded them offer them warm familiarity and support networks. This pattern applies as much to the Australian diaspora in London as it does to migrant communities in Melbourne. What's more, such community networks relieve state agencies of much work of immigrant absorption. That ethnic neighbourhoods persist well after the settlement of immigrant generations is also to be expected: after all, homes and businesses have been established, and a sense of community is at premium in mass societies. But the main reason why we should not concern ourselves with the fact of ethnic enclaves is that it is not the business of government, in a free society, to tell people in which residential areas they can live. Residential restrictions were the province of Nazi Germany and the Soviet Union, and, before them, of Tsarist Russia. Windschuttle, Pauline Hanson and others' itch to engineer residential patterns is what is dangerous to Australian values and way of life.

Ditto the question of intermarriage. Windschuttle cites data (from Bob Birrell) showing that among second-generation migrant groups, the Lebanese are distinctive in overwhelmingly still marrying their own.[19] They thus fail, he said, 'the most revealing test of immigrant integration'. While he should have noted that, by his own test, Australian multiculturalism has been a resounding success, with most groups intermarrying at high rates, the main problem is the standard itself.

Two centuries ago, Napoleon I made Jews' entitlement to citizenship conditional on how they responded to twelve questions, one of which was whether they would marry their Christian neighbours. The Jewish notables of Paris gave the Emperor the answer he wanted, and the Jews have continued to marry their own pretty much ever since.[20] In Australia, the Jewish intermarriage rate is estimated at 15–25 per cent, which is less than the 26–39 per cent range Windschuttle cites for the Lebanese, including Christians and Muslims.[21] Yet Australian Jews—who, in

Sydney and Melbourne, also tend to reside in particular areas—are often cited (by conservatives) as model minority citizens. So why should intermarriage be the litmus test of integration? Of course, the sociological claim is that intermarriage is a structural factor that helps shape people's values, which it doubtless does. But last time I looked, in a free society, who one marries was broadly a matter for the individual and not the state to determine. Indeed, the concern of liberal societies has been about *preventing* coercive marriages within some cultural minorities.

The only rightful test of integration is, or should be, whether you conduct yourself as a good citizen and abide by the rules. But this simple proposition is made so much more difficult to realise when public leaders and commentators instinctively add, 'And by the way, we will consider you good citizens when your group has made a notable contribution.' Or: 'We don't like where you are choosing to live and who you are choosing to marry.' For then, plainly, the message is that, for your lot, abiding by the rules is *not* enough.

But it gets worse.

As in other Western countries, cultural exclusion has been blatantly and continually expressed against Australian Muslims and Arabs by the media commentariat since the September 11 and Bali attacks. Here is Piers Akerman in Sydney's *Daily Telegraph* on 13 September 2001: 'How, for example, do Muslim residents in Australia differ in their views from those of the Taliban or others capable of ordering these atrocities?' Notice how Australian Muslims are treated as one, and are considered merely 'residents in Australia'. In the stroke of a key, Akerman thinks nothing of robbing 300,000 or so Australians of their citizenship and sense of belonging. Then attorney-general Philip Ruddock was invited to speak at a Sydney mosque to mark an important Islamic festival, and proceeded to lecture his audience on the need to be law-abiding. He then reportedly was at a loss to understand why his audience should be insulted by these remarks.[22] Little wonder that in some cases the message has been received and internalised: we Muslims, we Lebanese, are indeed foreigners here.

But it gets worse.

Multicultural policy proclaims, and Australian governments rightly stress, the importance of all Australians respecting our democratic traditions and institutions. And yet the Howard government was happy to rush through Parliament in late 2005, without adequate debate, anti-terror legislation that involves serious abridgement of democratic rights. Similarly, at the same time the Howard government was telling Muslims that they must abide by democratic norms, it was telling the Muslim and Indigenous communities who would represent them to the government. What kind of lesson in democracy is this? It teaches only that our much-trumpeted core values, our Anglo traditions of liberal democracy, are so important to us that our leaders don't give a damn about them when it suits them.

The same applies to our mythic national values. The US political philosopher Michael Walzer visited Australia for the first time in 2005. He reported on his observations in America's *Dissent* magazine, in part, as follows:

> When people talk about 'Australian values,' mateyness is what they mostly mean. Hence the first response of Australians when radical Islamic preachers told their young listeners that Muslims must choose only Muslim friends: 'That's not matey.' I think that's a pretty good response, though I should note that the… ruling Liberal Party is busily enacting a neoliberal program whose inegalitarian effects are also, definitely, not matey.[23]

Nor, I would add, has our recent treatment of asylum seekers been very matey. By what tortured logic did we honour our iconic principle of the 'fair go' by denying asylum to refugees from Saddam Hussein and the Taliban, against whom we went to war?

There is an awful lot of jingoism in the public insistence on respect for our core values. Perhaps cultural minorities might have an easier time observing accepted standards if they weren't so often *double* standards. It is the hypocritical application of our multiculturalism policies and democratic values that helps to alienate people, and cast them to the margins of society. This is where a sense of rejection and anger can boil over into the desire to strike back.

National Identity and Integration

Let me conclude by considering the question of whether we need a shared national identity as well as shared liberal democratic values—the other part of Albrechtsen's 'talk that applauds the majority culture'.

Many people worry that multiculturalism disunites Australian society. They argue that an immigration program that admits too much cultural diversity and a domestic policy of cultural recognition fragments the nation and undermines an identity that Australians share in common. Public debate mostly centres on the question of *which* values should be the basis of integration into the Australian community. I think Australian identity and integration also raise important questions of *where* and *when*.

For some people, the answer is simple. Some—let's call them cultural nationalists—believe that there is only one, typically Anglo-Celtic, way of being Australian, *and* that citizenship and government in general should be about insisting that all Australians conform to this way.[24] Others—let's call them post-nationalists—contest the idea of there being a distinctive Australian culture and identity.

They argue that Australian national identity and cohesion can only be about accepting a range of political—typically, liberal-democratic—values.[25] The mistake of many critics of multiculturalism is to equate it with the strictures of post-nationalism and to push cultural nationalism instead.

There is, however, a third and, I think, more realistic and sensible alternative. This position—which may be called liberal nationalism—holds that Australian national identity is multifaceted and occupies different domains. There are certain political values and aspects of Australian identity that are appropriate for citizenship and are duly the province of government, such as liberal democratic norms, the inculcation and transmission of a national language, the teaching of the nation's history, and the establishment of national institutions, holidays and memorials. But there are also aspects of national identity that properly belong in the realm of civil society and beyond the business of government, such as how people dress, what they call themselves, how they spend their leisure, in what languages they speak to each other, and even in what accent they speak their English. On the liberal nationalist model, Australian culture and identity are not denied; rather, their ambit is spread across different spheres and jurisdictions.[26]

This more circumscribed, liberal nationalist approach to national identity is perhaps nowhere better illustrated than in the first national multicultural policy statement. The

National Agenda for a Multicultural Australia (1989) acknowledges the importance of 'our British heritage' in helping 'to define us as Australian.' It emphasises that 'Multiculturalism does not entail a rejection of Australian values, customs and beliefs'. As part of a 'common core', it highlights the 'basic institutional framework of Australian society', including English as the national language, rule of law, democracy, freedom and tolerance of expression, equality of the sexes, and an 'overriding and unifying commitment to Australia'. It expressly *excludes* from the public definition of Australian identity ethnocultural aspects such as skin colour, style of dress, mode of worship, or other languages spoken. And it recognises that the 'Australian way of life' will evolve and change over time with the 'changing face of the Australian population', among other influences.[27]

The liberal nationalist approach to cultural diversity remains dominant in Australia, notwithstanding the new preference for the rubrics of 'citizenship' and 'integration' over 'multiculturalism'. Almost all the things now promoted in the guise of 'integration' are key parts of the national multicultural policy statements. And the new emphasis on English language proficiency and some knowledge of the Australian way of life is by no means inconsistent with those policy statements. There is no suggestion, for example, that migrants and their children should not speak foreign tongues *as well*, which was the case in the days of Australian assimilationism.

Words are important, and perhaps 'integration' better suits the times than does 'multiculturalism' as an overarching rubric. But this should not be allowed to obscure the fact that liberal multiculturalism, in general, and Australian multiculturalism, in particular, are, and always have been, about integration.

And herein lies the lesson. A shared national identity and sense of belonging are, indeed, crucial to the task of integrating a diverse population. But these things are multifaceted. Being schooled in the Ned Kelly legend and umpteen visits to see the Dog on the Tucker Box alone cannot do the work of integration. We must also attend to the myriad ways in which cultural minorities continue to be marginalised and alienated—*despite* our stated commitment to multiculturalism or integration. The surest way of integrating minorities is to ensure they have stable jobs, that they are accessing the available educational opportunities and support networks, and that they are made to feel genuinely welcome through appropriate rhetoric. In the name of liberal autonomy, equality, and justice—and thus of liberal multiculturalism—this also means trying to accommodate minority traditions where we can, and explaining where, perhaps, we cannot. If our aim is a secure, well-integrated, and free and fair Australian society, then we have some way to go on all these scores.

MONOCULTURALISM, MUSLIMS AND MYTH MAKING

Waleed Aly

WALEED ALY

is a lecturer in the School of Political and Social Inquiry at Monash University. He is the author of *People Like Us: How Arrogance Is Dividing Islam and the West*, and *What's Right: The Future of Conservatism in Australia (Quarterly Essay 37)*.

Until very recently, NatWest, one of Britain's biggest commercial banks, had an enduring devotion to piggy banks. You could tell by glancing at its advertising. Its savings account was spruiked by two of them, one pink, one richly golden. Their images adorned the walls of NatWest branches, enticing you with their competitive interest rates.

But for entertainment value, it is hard to go past NatWest's 2007 sponsorship of English cricket, which made the piggy bank an eclectic character: a disco-dancing, moon-walking cricket umpire declaring the dismissal of a batsman; a spectator announcing the tea break by drinking tea from a trough. There was also the 'Farmy Army', a cheering, oinking hoggery referencing England's famously vocal (and drunken) 'Barmy Army'.[1] The animated pigs were cute, entertaining and everywhere.

How could this have been? I ask because the *Lancashire Evening Telegraph* reported in October 2005 that NatWest piggy banks had been removed from branches in East Lancashire 'in case they cause offence to Muslim customers'.[2] Three days later the *Daily Express* ran the story on its front page under the enormous headline: 'HOGWASH: Now the PC brigade bans piggy banks in case they upset Muslims',[3] only this time, it had been elevated to a 'decision by high street banks' and was condemned more colourfully as 'barmy' and 'bonkers'. Quotes were sourced from commentators in disparate parts of the country, creating the impression of a nationwide scandal, which the newspaper explained in scriptural terms: 'All promotional material bearing the figure has now been scrapped because the Koran forbids Muslims from eating pork and pigs are considered by them to be unclean.'

Australian newspapers particularly lapped it up. The story ran in the *Daily Telegraph*, the *Mercury*, the *Advertiser*, the *NT News*, the *Newcastle Herald* and the *Courier-Mail*, as well as online at the websites of Channel Nine, the *Age* and the *Sydney Morning Herald*.[4] The *Daily Telegraph*'s version had banks not merely withdrawing piggy banks from advertising, but no longer giving them to children.[5] It set talkback radio predictably alight, with callers warning gravely of how 'the Muslim world is starting to control our thinking and actually our lives'.[6] But lest it be thought such hysteria was merely the domain of the talkback demographic, here is the Very Reverend Christopher

Armstrong, Dean of Blackburn: 'The next thing we will be banning Christmas trees and cribs and the logical result of that process is a bland uniformity.'[7]

Yet the NatWest piggies persisted. They did so because the story was fabricated. 'There is absolutely no fact in the story,' NatWest's Media Relations Manager told the ABC's *Media Watch*. 'Piggy banks have been and will continue to be used as a promotional item by NatWest.'[8] The same cannot be said of Halifax, the other major British bank implicated in the report. 'We no longer have any advertising that features piggy banks or is piggy bank related,' its spokesperson told the *Lancashire Evening Telegraph*. That much is true. But Halifax hasn't used piggy banks for years. This was a decision of advertising strategy[9] that had nothing to do with Muslims at all.

This kind of fictional news story should be the rarest of exceptions. But it is not, and where Muslims are concerned, it is becoming something of an emerging genre. British journalists Peter Oborne and James Jones catalogue several examples of these, drawing on a study performed by the Cardiff School of Journalism, Media and Cultural Studies. Here is a brief edited summary published in the *Independent*:

> '"Muslim Sickos" Maddie Kidnap Shock'—*Daily Star*, 28 April 2008. The story did not, as readers might have inferred from the front-page headline,

reveal that Madeleine McCann had been kidnapped by a 'Muslim sicko'. In fact, it refers to a [Muslim] website on which claims were made that Madeleine's parents were involved in her disappearance.

'Get off my bus I need to pray'—the *Sun*, 28 March 2008. This was the story of a Muslim bus driver ordering his passengers off his bus so that he could pray. The *Sun* story, along with footage of the bus driver praying, was widely circulated around right-wing blogs. Dhimmi Watch, the right-wing blog on the site Jihad Watch that catalogues perceived outrages committed by Muslims, even included the *Sun* story in their 'ever-expanding You Can't Make This Stuff Up file'. Well, actually, you can. The bus had been delayed, so in order to maintain frequency the bus company had ordered the driver to stop his bus and allow passengers to board the bus behind. Tickets and CCTV evidence show that all the passengers were on that bus within a minute.

The so-called witness, a 21-year-old plumber who recorded the bus driver praying, had not been on the bus, and had arrived after the incident to find a small crowd outside a bus.

'The crescent and the canteen'—the *Economist*, 19 October 2006. There was no truth in the article's suggestion that Leicester University had banned pork

> on campus. In actual fact, the university Student Union had made just one out of the numerous cafes on campus halal, in a decision which had as much to do with economic factors as cultural sensitivity as Leicester has a large number of Muslim students. The other 26 cafes on the campus, including the main canteen, were still serving pork as usual.[10]

Other examples could be cited in this connection that hold Muslims falsely responsible for an impressive range of social crimes from banning Christmas to risking the lives of hospital patients with unprofessional hygiene standards and mob violence against returned British soldiers.[11] The connecting thread barely needs articulation: Muslim minorities constitute a threat to the Western way of life by seeking aggressively to impose their norms onto the majority, and displace Western (in these cases, British) culture in the process. Of course, intensified scrutiny of Western Muslims is not incomprehensible in the post-September 11 era, and especially after the 7/7 bombings on the London Underground, the perpetrators of which were raised in Britain. Nevertheless this begs a simple question: if Muslims are so obviously threatening, why the need to make things up about them?

Ultimately it is a matter of narrative. In a sense, these fictional stories exist because a particular conspiratorial worldview, present among some commentators and newspaper editors, demands they do. Terrorism may have triggered and even legitimised the paranoia associated with this vision, but these narratives transcend issues of political violence and physical security. Terrorism is only one of a range of news events conscripted into the service of a *cultural* discourse. It is not that Muslims are necessarily terrorists (though the theme is never far away). It is that they, at least to the extent they are newsworthy, are a kind of cultural cancer: a foreign body whose presence in the host organ may fatally undermine it. A Cardiff University study is instructive in this connection. It found that the number of reports in the British print news media concerning the religious and cultural issues associated with Muslims had now overtaken the number about terrorism.[12] Such culture-based stories were a comparatively insignificant component of the British print media landscape as recently as 2002. It is a growth area, reflective of a growing discourse.

I do not mean to convey that every such news report is imagined or exaggerated. Many are not. But the social discourses that feast so gleefully on this news have now gained such momentum that they generate their own grist. Such fabrications and distortions, then, are ultimately symptomatic of a polemical social mood.

Here, we can observe the textbook definition of a moral panic manifesting itself. Consider Stanley Cohen's classic description:

> A condition, episode, person or group of person emerges to become defined as a threat to societal values or interests; its nature is presented in a stylised and stereotypical fashion by the mass media; the moral barricades are manned by editors, bishops, politicians and other right-thinking people; socially accredited experts pronounce their diagnoses and solutions...Sometimes the object of the panic is quite novel and at other times it is something which has been in existence long enough, but suddenly appears in the limelight. Sometimes the panic passes over and is forgotten, except in folklore and collective memory; at other times it has more serious and long-lasting repercussions and might produce such changes as those in legal and social policy or even in the way society conceives itself.[13]

Of course, as Cohen's schema makes clear, no moral panic is possible without its 'folk devils': those held responsible for deviant behaviour, who emerge into the public space cast involuntarily in a villainous role. They are, in Sean Hier's phrase, 'stripped of all positive characteristics and endowed with pejorative evaluations'.[14] Of course, the identity of these devils varies naturally with time and place. We have long been familiar with this phenomenon. Whether it be Asian immigrants, welfare cheats, uncontrollable delinquent youth, or, once upon a time, Catholics, folk devils are a constant of public life. Their presence seems the necessary lubricant for public debate.

So today's moral panic surrounds the Muslim folk devil. Note how a relatively trivial event (or tale)—like the retirement of piggy banks—is magnified to the point of front-page tabloid outrage. In this terrain, the normal rules of media prioritisation seem suspended: truly sensational news defers to the apparently trivial; foreign stories trump local ones. Why? Because the *narratives* that surround the story are more sensational and localised than the stories they appropriate. Newsworthiness resides, not in the literal copy, but in its constructed context.

Allow the cabbies of Minnesota to demonstrate. The Minneapolis-St Paul International Airport is serviced by 900 taxi divers, around three quarters of whom are Somali Muslims. In October 2006 the *Australian* reported that these drivers had 'declared jihad on duty-free, refusing to carry passengers who are carrying alcohol'.[15] It is difficult to assess the genuine significance of the story. On one hand, an airport spokesman explained that these refusals had 'slowly grown over the years to the point that it's become a significant customer service issue for us'. On the other, airport commission statistics showed that of the 120,000 taxi rides from the airport in a two-month period, there were some twenty-seven refusals—about 0.02 per cent.[16] Whatever the case, the story, taken in isolation, was of limited gravity to an Australian audience. The same could not be said for the story, that broke only two days prior, that a bullet was fired into a Perth mosque while 400 people were worshipping, narrowly missing women and children.[17] That was both local and sensational.

The *Australian* failed to report the mosque shooting. Yet it found the Minnesotan story sufficiently significant to warrant both front-page exposure and an editorial. And it is in the editorial that the reason for its prominence was made plain:

> What is happening at the airport in Minneapolis-St. Paul is just as much of an indictment of multiculturalism as other incidences of self-censorship and self-flagellation that occur on a near-daily basis among Westerners seeking to avoid or atone for offending the most prudish or outlandish of Islamic sensibilities. And it shows what can happen when a culture allows immigrants to behave as conquerors, instead of politely but firmly suggesting that newcomers who wish to impose their theocratic ways on a secular community try their luck elsewhere.[18]

An attempt to cause grievous bodily harm to Muslims in prayer simply does not feed an established media narrative. It remains an isolated incident of no enduring relevance or concern. But when a cluster of Somali taxi drivers refuse to transport alcohol for clients, a prevalent discourse is reactivated. It becomes another instalment in a series of 'incidences of self-censorship and self-flagellation' on the part of Westerners who are over-tolerant of the restrictive idiosyncrasies of Muslim migrants. It is, above all, an 'indictment of multiculturalism'. And indeed, the *Australian* has expended impressive energy running the prosecution. Only three weeks later, it editorialised even more forthrightly on the 'veiled conceit of multiculturalism' in the following terms:

> Many Britons are concerned that multicultural policies that have discouraged assimilation have divided their society and created what one commentator called a 'voluntary apartheid'.
>
> While tolerance is certainly a positive virtue that should be strived for, it cannot be a cultural suicide pact. A culture that is tolerant of those who are intolerant of its freedoms is ripe for destruction, and bit by bit will see all it [sic] values eroded. And radical Islam knows this.[19]

This essay is not principally concerned with matters of media malpractice, but with the socio-political narratives that proceed from them: narratives of a Western culture besieged by the descending Muslim hordes, who exploit the 'cultural suicide pact' of multiculturalism: that is to say the most recent and popular incarnation of anti-multiculturalist discourse, which has asserted itself most energetically in the aftermath of the London bombings. As we shall see, it is a discourse steeped in mythology. We might expect Muslims to be the subject of this mythology, a phenomenon that will duly be explored. But as Hier reminds us:

> ...although moral panics center on a particular folk devil, the locus of the panic is not the object of its symbolic resonances, not the folk devil itself. Rather, folk devils serve as the ideological embodiment of deeper anxieties, perceived of as 'a problem' only in and through social definition and construction.[20]

This suggests that to the extent it follows the logic of moral panic, contemporary railing against multiculturalism is a product of deeper identity politics that ultimately have little to do with Muslims themselves. If so, we may predict that any associated myth making is not only about Muslims, but about the culture ostensibly being defended against them. This essay aims to demonstrate this and to conclude that while anti-multiculturalism condemns a policy that it perceives has been raised disastrously to the level of a political ideology, it produces a political ideology of its own: monoculturalism.

But first, a word on what this essay is not. It is not a defence (or even an evaluation) of multiculturalism. That sort of discussion can be found elsewhere in this volume. For the purposes of disclosure, I confess that I am sympathetic to multiculturalism, though this depends significantly on how one chooses to define and give expression to it. (I do not, for instance, support any articulation of multiculturalism that requires absolute cultural relativism—assuming such an articulation exists). What follows is a separate inquiry that is not so much concerned with the fact of anti-multiculturalism, as the reasoning that supports it.

The Popular Anti-Multiculturalist Narrative

It is possible to object to multiculturalism on a range of diverse grounds. Zygmunt Bauman, for example, criticises it on essentially cosmopolitan grounds, arguing that it offers only 'negative' rather than 'positive' recognition: that is basic tolerance, rather than equal participation.[21] Johann Hari objects to it on the basis (among others) that it artificially deems minority cultures to be monolithic, static artefacts in a manner that denies people their individual agency.[22] This is quite different from criticising multiculturalism as an assault on the majority. In short, the fact that someone opposes multiculturalism does not immediately reveal their political orientations or their reasoning. There is not one single anti-multicultural narrative. There are several, with varying degrees of overlap. But it is a fair assumption that the media performances encountered above outline the basic thrust of the most dominant, popular expression of anti-multiculturalism, certainly in Australia and probably throughout the Western world. To be sure, a comprehensive survey of objections to multiculturalism is beyond the size constraints of this essay. Accordingly, for present purposes it should suffice to engage with a broadly representative version of this popular anti-multiculturalist narrative.

That narrative has been introduced above in short form. But it deserves to be rendered in more detail here, so we can more subtly appreciate its key characteristics. And here, perhaps quintessentially, stands Melanie Phillips' *Londonistan*.[23] Her discussion will be used as a representative touchstone for the purposes of analysis in this essay. Even though her focus is on Britain, many of her arguments are replicated, often in precise terms, by Australia's most strident anti-multiculturalists. In fact it represents probably the fullest expression of popular anti-multiculturalism found in Australia. Phillips devotes an entire chapter of the book to the emphatic excoriation of multiculturalism,[24] which she defines as 'the doctrine that...holds that Britain is now made up of many cultures that are all equal and therefore have to be treated in an identical fashion, and that any attempt to impose the majority culture over those of minorities is by definition racist'.[25] It is a questionable definition—almost a straw man—but we can accept it for the purposes of this analysis.

Her basic argument is frankly apocalyptic: through multiculturalism, British culture has completely surrendered itself to the politics of minority separateness that has nurtured nothing less than radical Islamism. Britain, then, is 'paralysed by a multicultural threat it cannot even bring itself to name'.[26] Its very survival is precarious both physically and culturally and multiculturalism is to blame.

For Phillips, the twin scourges of relativism and postmodernism laid the foundation for this. Together with the collapse of the British Empire and post-colonial guilt, they conspired to reduce British culture to a nullity. In its place emerged the 'revolutionary ideology of the left' during the 1960s and 70s which shattered the moral assumptions of society.[27] Hippies destroyed Britain.

The alleged result was a cultural vacuum into which marched assertive, corrosive minorities. 'Multiculturalism and antiracism were now the weapons with which minorities were equipped to beat the majority,' Phillips asserts,[28] making plain what she means in the following passage:

> Britain…has effectively allowed itself to be taken hostage by militant gays, feminists or 'anti-racists' who used weapons such as public vilification, moral blackmail and threats to people's livelihoods to force the majority to give in to their demands. And those demands were identical to those made by the Islamists: not merely to tolerate their values as minority rights but to replace normative values altogether and subordinate the values of the majority to the minority, because majority values set up a

> hierarchy that is deemed to be innately discriminatory. So when Muslims refused to accept minority status and insisted instead that their values must trump those of the majority, Britain had no answer.[29]

It is perhaps a more sophisticated articulation of Jerry Falwell's infamous diagnosis that pagans, abortionists, feminists, civil libertarians, gays and lesbians 'helped [the September 11 attacks] happen'.[30] Phillips merely omits the dimension of divine punishment from her analysis.

The point for Phillips is that minorities, specifically migrants and especially Muslims, need to be told how to behave. Left to their own devices—or worse, invited to retain their cultural identities—they will proceed disastrously to inflict their backward cultures on the majority. So, says Phillips, Muslims commenced 'campaigning for public recognition of their religious agenda by the state'. They sought to establish their own schools, and demanded halal meat in others. They sought separate education for girls, and burned copies of *The Satanic Verses* to coerce the British government into banning Salman Rushdie's book.[31] No doubt the lynch-mob behaviour of these last protests were irredeemably contemptible, as was that which surrounded the Danish cartoon imbroglio of 2006. But why should this be lumped together with a desire for halal meat in schools or Islamic private schools as some kind of cultural invasion? There is nothing in the majority British culture

Phillips so venerates that precludes the consumption of halal meat. Its impact on majority culture is little to none.

Similarly, non-Muslim (and especially Christian) faith schools are common in Britain. Where is Phillips' rage towards Britain's Jewish schools? Or does she deny they exist? After all, she makes plain that British Jews are an exceptional minority because they were always considered too privileged to be allowed to benefit from multicultural largesse.[32] Presumably, then, they never campaigned for 'public recognition of their religious agenda by the state'. Are we to conclude that they never sought to establish their own schools? Or is that only an act of cultural aggression when Muslims do it?

It surely cannot be that Britain's Jewish schools are necessarily more demographically inclusive. Certainly, some are spectacularly so, like Birmingham's King David School, about half of whose students are Muslims. (How confounding it must be for Phillips to discover Muslim students—whose mothers mostly wear the hijab and are reportedly devout—who learn modern Hebrew, celebrate Israeli Independence Day and recite Jewish prayers!)[33] But if this is Phillips' reasoning, will she similarly condemn the Jewish school that refused to admit a child because his mother was not born a Jew?[34] It doesn't particularly fuss me, but then, I don't consider the establishment of religious private schools by minorities a form of cultural invasion.

Or perhaps Phillips' complaints are ultimately about terrorism. After all, the logical extension of this is that 'multiculturalism has unwittingly fomented Islamic radicalism in the sacred cause of "diversity"'.[35] So maybe the difference is that Jews don't detonate bombs on London public transport. True. But then again, neither do all but four British Muslims, none of whom attended a British Islamic school. In fact it is difficult to identify even a single Western Muslim terrorist who attended an Islamic private school in the West. Typically the story of radicalisation has been one that climaxes around the age of tertiary education and has nothing to do with secondary-school brainwashing. Indeed most who turn to violence have a comparatively shallow history of religiosity. Their teen years are more likely to have been substantially irreligious.

Such double standards seem to be a regular feature of popular anti-multiculturalism, a fact exposed in Australia with the emergence of the Exclusive Brethren. The Howard Government had been sceptical of what it termed 'zealous multiculturalism'.[36] It famously dropped the phrase 'multicultural affairs' from the relevant government department.[37] It instituted citizenship tests to require migrants to learn the English language, Australian history and Australian values.[38] Indeed, as Prime Minister, John Howard had an unabashed emphasis on values: Muslims were often commanded to integrate, which 'means accepting Australian values' such as 'the equality of men and women'.[39] The Exclusive Brethren confounded this. News reports depicted this Christian sect shunning democracy to the extent that it forbade voting. It shunned non-believers, requiring its members to avoid conversation with them, and was prepared to separate children from parents if necessary. It shunned university education.[40] It protected men who were convicted of sexually abusing young girls, and vandalised the homes of those bringing the charges.[41] Its women were commanded to wear long, loose-fitting clothes.[42] It flouted court orders.[43] In short, it rejected such well-rehearsed Australian values as democracy, the rule of law, gender equality and tolerance, and it certainly rejected integration. Yet, the values-promoting Prime Minister not only refrained from lecturing this sect on integration, he repeatedly met with its members, while his party benefited from Exclusive Brethren donations.[44] When pressed on this, John Howard remarked that 'it's a free country... and they were not breaking the law'.[45] Which is as true for the Exclusive Brethren is it is for Muslims—whether they speak English or not.[46]

There are several curious features of Phillips' anti-multicultural analysis that render it ambiguous, even incongruous. 'Muslims regard Western values as an assault on Islamic principles,' she declares,[47] echoing the assumption popular among Western politicians that terrorists are motivated by a hatred of the Western way of life. Yet Phillips has just finished making the case that Western values have been sacrificed to the cult of multiculturalism, relativised out of meaningful existence. 'Britain,' she bemoans, 'has become a largely post-Christian society, where traditional morality has been systematically undermined and replaced by an "anything goes" culture.'[48] Precisely which 'Western values', then, do Muslims regard as an 'assault'? Or do they take umbrage at the postmodern absence of values in the West? If so, Phillips might consider joining them.

There is something vaguely paradoxical at work here. If recalcitrant minorities fume violently at values that allegedly no longer exist, the solution, it seems, is to enforce conformity with shared values in the defence of liberal democracy. It is a mind-bending prescription. An inescapable implication of liberalism is the individual's freedom of thought. That means nothing if it does not permit the individual to subscribe to dissenting value systems that may even be repugnant to the majority, just as freedom of speech means nothing without the freedom to offend. The liberal democratic state may well reflect one set of cultural norms over another—through its use of an official language and its marking of particular national days, for instance—but it does not seek to prescribe or determine the personal values of its citizens. Its values are primarily *institutional*: the rule of law, freedom of speech and conscience. It has no interest in intervening until the law is breached, and it does not use the law as a means of implementing mass culture. That is, it potentially leads us to something like the position John Howard articulated with regard to the Exclusive Brethren. Until the law turns to something like legalising behaviour that harms other individuals, such as honour killings—which it simply will never do—there should be no existential crisis for liberal democracy.

Yet many anti-multiculturalists too easily resort to a kind of groupism, prosecuting an identity politics of collectivism. Muslims and other minorities are clustered together and judged on the basis of their group membership. Generalisations are made about their values and attitudes quite inconsistently with liberalism's axiomatic individualism. Simultaneously, a majority group is constructed whose values are determined for it by the declaration of an elite. So, for example, we have Patrick O'Flynn of the *Daily Express* telling Channel 4: 'The wider population is beginning to say, "Well actually, we've had enough of this; *we* feel aggrieved; *we* feel that many of the values we've always lived by in this country are under threat, and *you lot are threatening them*".'[49] As we have seen, Phillips is anxious that minorities know their place; that they understand they are minorities and behave as such. That reveals a collectivist instinct. Should she not be apprehending them as individual citizens?

As Geoffrey Brahm Levey observes, multiculturalism in Australia has proceeded from the assumptions of liberalism:

> Australian multicultural policy is highly individualistic...It is each individual who enjoys the rights (such as those to cultural identity and respect, and access to equity) and bears the responsibilities (of abiding by Australia's liberal democratic institutions) under the policy. Lest there be any ambiguity, the *National Agenda* goes on to state that: 'Fundamentally, multiculturalism is about the rights of the individual'.[50]

This does not mean multiculturalism is liberalism's necessary logical extension. Certainly, liberalism should have no quibble with the presence of several cultures within a single society, but it may quite plausibly object to a state policy of multiculturalism on the ground that the state should engage with citizens as individuals, rather than as members of a cultural group. The *Australian*'s Janet Albrechtsen mounts precisely this argument: 'it's time for our political leaders to stop engaging with Muslims as Muslims', she writes. 'They are citizens; no special rules apply.'[51] Yet she applauds when they engage with Muslims—specifically and exclusively so—where that engagement takes the form of outlining for them which personal values they must accept.[52] Of course it is true that values are critically important to society, for it could scarcely exist without them. But if values are to be promoted within the framework of liberalism, they are not the stuff of government declaration and should not be articulated in group terms. This government performance Albrechtsen so admires is ultimately an illiberal one. It is not one whereby the government stresses Muslims' standing in society as individuals—which seems at best to be her starting point. It is not demanding Muslims think of themselves civically as individuals. It is doing the opposite: addressing and conceiving of them as a collective for the purpose of demanding conformity with a collective majority.

So the groupist orientation of much anti-multiculturalist discourse, often from those who champion liberalism, presents an intriguing tension. It suggests there might be something more at play than the dispassionate application of a political philosophy. The double standards identified above also point to something of a parochial streak. There are plenty of non-Muslim Australians whose personal values are affronting to the majority. Often they form religious or political groups. Yet they are rarely chosen for some kind of public, group-based values education—or even values education at all.

In this narrative there are, ultimately, those who belong and those who do not, and in any such dynamic, the rhetorical field is vulnerable to a substantial dose of mythology. Indeed, the examples already canvassed of media fabrication and distortion indicate that the myth-making process, at least to the extent it concerns Muslims, is well underway.

Anti-Multiculturalism and the Mythical Muslim

Implicit in much of the above is a conflation. Discrete issues—for example faith-based schooling and terrorism—become rhetorically fused in a single, groupist narrative. This is presented as if there is no *conceptual* difference between the Muslim requesting halal catering and the one who aims to bomb Britain into an Islamic pseudo-theocracy. To the extent these social menaces differ, they differ only in *degree*. One adopts a more violent methodology than the other but both are presented as though they are vanguards of the same cause: a cultural war determined to displace the dominant culture by whatever means are available. In this way, the trivial story is projected hysterically onto the largest available screen, often the front page. As we have seen, sometimes these reports are simply fabricated—indeed, Phillips relies on the piggy-bank story in support of her argument[53]—but this is not necessary. It is sufficient that that they fit the narrative being constructed. So from our breakfast tables in Australia we are invited to bristle at a handful of taxi drivers in Minnesota, in the belief that they signify an existential threat. The fact that Western societies have precisely nothing to fear from, say, halal or, similarly, kosher food being served in school cafeterias is completely submerged by a discourse of cultural panic. All evidences crisis.

The associated vision of Muslims is, quite obviously, an unflattering one. Here, Muslims are monolithic, belong to unchanging cultures, and are intolerant of pluralism and dispute. They subjugate women. They use their faith mainly for political purposes and for strategic and military advantage, and have made no meaningful contributions to debates on Western liberalism, modernity or secularism. Islam itself is a successor to Nazism and communism. Moreover, Phillips boldly generalises this dystopian portrait, insisting that all of the 'assertions about Muslims in this list are without exception true, at least in part'. Meanwhile, only a 'small minority in Britain are horrified' by all of these attitudes, while 'a troubling number...subscribe to all of them and the majority subscribe to at least some'. She demonstrates none of this, of course. Phillips merely asserts it as unimpeachable fact, warning that any denial of its truth 'displays a spectacular proclivity towards national suicide'.[54]

Thus does Phillips see a marauding aggressive minority which, like its medieval forebears, is bent on conquest. For her, this is apparently some kind of coordinated scheme for cultural and political domination: 'jihadi Islamism...has become today the dominant strain within the Islamic world,' she asserts without any empirical evidence to support such a startling claim.[55] She estimates that 'hundreds of thousands' of British Muslims—from a population nearing two million—'lead law-abiding lives and merely want to prosper and raise their families in peace'. That is to say a majority do not. On this score, Phillips probably goes further than most of her fellow anti-multiculturalists who deploy safer caveats about a 'moderate' majority. But her general characterisation of the Muslim minority has broader support:

> The attempt to establish this separate Muslim identity is growing more and more intense, with persistent pressure for official recognition of Islamic family law, the rise of a de facto parallel Islamic legal system not recognised by the state, demands for highly politicised Islamic dress codes, prayer meetings or halal food to be provided by schools and other institutions, and so on. No other minority attempts to impose its values on the host society like this.[56]

Really? Official recognition of a parallel religious legal system governing areas of family law (and commercial matters) is what British Jews already have in the form of the *Beth Din*—which is backed by no less than an Act of Parliament.[57] Perhaps other minorities have not attempted to secure 'prayer meetings' (whatever that means), but we do know that Jewish students have demanded—perfectly reasonably—that exams be shifted so they can observe the Sabbath, even being prepared to resort to legal action to ensure it.[58] Phillips does not make clear precisely what she means by 'highly politicised Islamic dress codes', but if she is referring to various forms of veiling, it is an absurd argument. This is partly because Phillips has simply deemed veiling to be politicised when there is no reason this must necessarily be the case—and little evidence that it is for most British Muslim women.[59] It is a religious mode of dress, and Muslims are far from alone in seeking the right to wear religious items in schools. For example, a Sikh girl in Wales took her school to the High Court for suspending her because she wore a religious bangle. Some twenty-five years previously, a Sikh boy took similar action against a school that tried to force him to cut his hair and remove his turban.[60] And precisely how consistently does Phillips maintain that Muslims are the most aggressively imposing minority? What about the militant gays, feminists and 'anti-racists' whose demands, you will recall, 'were identical to those made by the Islamists'?

It is apparent that Phillips views Muslims, and 'multicultural' British society generally, through thoroughly jaundiced lenses. For her, multicultural relativism has so completely eviscerated British values and identity, so unremittingly sanctified minority cultures beyond censure, that it is no longer possible to criticise Muslims:

> Multiculturalism...forbade criticism of Muslim practices such as forced marriages or polygamy...Even to draw attention to such practices was to be labelled a racist. After all, were not these customs now said to be morally equal to British traditions, such as equal rights for women and the protection of children's educational interests?[61]

The suggestion that Muslims are now above criticism because of a multicultural orthodoxy that prevails 'throughout all the institutions of British public life'[62] is not merely a wild overstatement. It is among the more perverse fantasies circulating in the mainstream Western public conversation. A Cardiff University study identified that 69 per cent of stories about Muslims in the British press since 2000 represent Muslims as a 'source of problems or in opposition to traditional British culture', while only 5 per cent of stories 'were based on attacks on or problems *for* British Muslims'.[63] The trend is echoed in the findings of a 2007 study that of all the articles about Muslims in a news week chosen at random, 4 per cent were 'positive', 5 per cent were 'neutral', and a staggering 91 per cent were 'negative'.[64] Even if we assume—perhaps charitably—that none of these articles was in any way fabricated, distorted or exaggerated and that all were entirely newsworthy, it is clear that most of these 'institutions of British public life' feel no reluctance at all to 'draw attention' to negative aspects of Muslim behaviour. This includes such publications as the *Independent* and the *Guardian* which Phillips would likely regard as paragons of political correctness and multicultural orthodoxy.[65] Indeed, as Peter Oborne and James Jones have observed, the preparedness to criticise Muslims and Islam proudly is alive and well across the political spectrum. After noting rather forthright examples from a range of British commentators and novelists, they conclude that the record demonstrates 'the power of Islamophobia to unite public culture at every level. It is not just confined to so-called tabloid newspapers. It is to be found in the broadsheets as well.'[66] Perhaps the most startling example they cite comes from Polly Toynbee, 'normally regarded as a model of political correctness'[67] who declares 'I am an Islamophobe, and proud of it'.[68] Not much multicultural reticence there.

Perhaps Phillips is right to assume some will deem Toynbee racist. Toynbee herself assumes the same.[69] But that fact, on its own, is of unclear significance. Many others will either cheer her on or say nothing. It is deeply implausible to argue anti-Muslim rhetoric is being silenced. Toynbee remains one of the *Guardian*'s most prominent and influential columnists. The same is true of Phillips and the *Daily Mail*. Indeed several of the Western world's most prominent (and promoted) writers and columnists are of a similar view: Mark Steyn, Robert Spencer and Oriana Fallaci are but a few. This is some strange brand of censorship.

Two clarifications at this point are in order. First, nothing in this essay argues that all Muslims are entirely blameless, that there are no causes for concern or that all criticism of Muslims should be treated with suspicion or as evidence of rank prejudice. Some Muslims—perhaps as many as 4000 in the United Kingdom—present a genuine security risk.[70] Some Muslims do make unreasonable demands of dubious necessity, ostensibly in the name of their beliefs—Minnesotan taxi drivers among them. Some social tensions do exist in Western societies between Muslims and non-Muslims to which Muslims are contributing. Not all anxieties are necessarily disingenuous. But this does not avoid the fact that the anti-multiculturalist narrative—represented here by Phillips—constructs a moral panic on the back of the Muslim 'folk devil'. As Domonic Bearfield reminds us, 'although the folk devil is a product of social construction, one should not conclude that it is wholly fantasy or make believe'.[71] Moral panics usually proceed from a kernel of truth. It is just that the sense of the threat is often misplaced and the scope of it exaggerated to the point of deception.

Second, no argument is being made here that

Western societies are uniformly, invariably and in every particular prejudiced against Muslims. Societies are a collection of complex currents and countercurrents, such that almost anything can be found within them. The studies cited in this chapter, for example, are proof that within government and mainstream media there are many who take the construction of the Muslim 'folk devil' seriously enough to devote considerable resources to exposing and confronting it. Indeed Phillips' own newspaper, the *Daily Mail*, published a lengthy feature by Peter Oborne to this effect.[72] Meanwhile, for all the criticism it has received, multiculturalism retains majority support in Britain[73] and even more emphatically in Australia.[74] The anti-multiculturalist narrative is clearly a minority worldview even if that minority is significant. This essay is concerned with assessing that narrative, not with passing any judgment on societies more broadly. And since it is a narrative that asserts, in part, that Muslims are fraudulently and uncritically protected from reasonable criticism by a pervasive orthodoxy of political correctness, it is necessary to point out that large sectors of public discourse prove the opposite: that it is now possible 'to make broad and deeply insulting generalisations about Muslims of a kind that would simply be impossible to make about any other minority group'.[75] Indeed, this is often justified on the grounds that no other minority group is remotely as threatening. The circle completes itself.

Still, this Muslim exceptionalism is only half the story. There is some truth to the observation that myth making about Islam and Muslims has a long Western history of which today's mythology is the latest instalment.[76] But the popular anti-multiculturalist narrative leaves us clues that suggest a broader rhetorical game. Phillips' argument, for example, traverses extraordinary breadth, much of which has nothing directly to do with Muslims: internationalism and human rights law are similarly lashed.[77] A similar tendency is visible in the *Australian*'s criticisms of 'inner-city postmodernists and progressives' in editorialising in the area.[78] This places us squarely in the culture wars, in which Muslims are largely rhetorical pawns. This suggests that, at the very deepest level, the debate about multiculturalism is not about Muslims, even if it seems unhealthily preoccupied with them. Rather, it is about the dominant culture. This observation has a symmetry about it that makes perfect intuitive sense. To construct an ideal outsider is in fact to construct one's self. The relationship is symbiotic.

This is perfectly consistent with Hier's observations about the role of the folk devil. It exists not merely for its own sake, but as a means of allowing us to engage with deeper anxieties. If it is true that much popular anti-multiculturalist discourse fashions a mythical Muslim, then the corollary is that it generates a similar mythology about the besieged dominant culture.

Making the Mythical Us

In any essentialised criticism of a social out-group there is another unstated message being communicated: that those criticisms do not apply to *us*. To berate Muslims for intolerance, militancy or misogyny is simultaneously to celebrate the majority's tolerance, peacefulness and gender equity. It is both an admonition and an exoneration. Understanding this helps explain why, in James Button's words, 'responses to Islam confound old distinctions of left and right. A conservative Dutch Government is insisting that would-be Muslim migrants recognise the Netherlands' commitment to feminism and gay rights before they come'.[79] Indeed it is precisely in the interests of a conservative politician to do so. In appropriating these causes they can celebrate them as achievements, rather than as ongoing struggles. This leaves them complete such that the conservative need take no further action. As long as Muslims remain central, villainous characters in the values conversation, any progressive attack is blunted. The conservative politician can retort compellingly: 'we are not misogynists and homophobes—*they* are!' It has become a common rhetorical feature. Said John Howard:

> ...in certain areas, such as the equality of men and women, the societies that some people have left were not as contemporary and as progressive as ours is. And I think people who come from societies where women are treated in an inferior fashion have to learn very quickly that that is not the case in Australia. That men and women do have equality and they're each entitled to full respect.[80]

In what other context would Howard celebrate the idea that Australia is 'contemporary and progressive'? And who, in this context, can disagree? No doubt, many feminists will contest the assertion that 'men and women do have equality' in Australia, but when the conversation is shifted to a relative one juxtaposing Muslims, any such argument is unsustainable and therefore lost.

And so a heroic self-image is gradually constructed: an ideal self where all vice has been exported onto a demonic other. The constructed foe, then, depends on who we need ourselves to be. The welfare cheat affirms us as honest and hardworking. The uncontrollable adolescent reassures us of the competence of our own parenting. So, as Meyda Yegenoglu observes, the veiled Muslim woman was once an untamed seductress, drawing animalistic, lustful men into grave sin. That was the view of a virtuous, sexually proper Europe.[81] Today she is a symbol of oppression for a free West, or even a symbol of violent radicalism for a

West that is peace-loving (since its many wars are without exception noble and unavoidable rather than self-interested and plundering). This cloth is a flexible symbol indeed.

The self need never be engaged critically in this process. It is simply venerated. This is self-affirmation by declaration. Its relationship to history can, of course, be casual. Thus it becomes entirely possible even for German politicians to talk to its minorities as if the Holocaust never happened. Recall the case of Ashkan Dejegah, a footballer who plays for Germany but also holds an Iranian passport. Dejegah refused to travel with the team to play against Israel, not as a matter of ideological conviction, but for fear that he would be barred entry to Iran in future. German outrage was understandably palpable, but Christian Democrats general secretary Ronald Pofalla's choice of words was instructively poor: 'Whoever represents Germany, whether he be a native German or an immigrant, has to identify with the history and culture of our society'.[82] Given the 'history and culture' of twentieth-century Germany, this is the darkest of ironies.

The invocation of history in this context is far from exceptional. Indeed much popular anti-multiculturalism relies on presenting the besieged majority as the guardians of history and tradition. The sub-text is hardly subtle: that it is Muslims (or migrants generally) who have brought these vices with them. Hence their exceptionalism. There is something unique about their presence that threatens an unprecedented cultural fracture. The past was certain, confident and good.

Which returns us to Phillips. A key assumption of her analysis is that Britain's traditional policy of assimilation expressed and emerged from a 'robust sense of pride in its national culture and history'. Multiculturalism is therefore the product of 'a series of developments [that] shattered Britain's confidence in its own integrity and, deeper still, its very sense of what the nation was'.[83] This necessarily implies—though Phillips says it explicitly—that 'until about forty years ago, British society had been relatively homogeneous...British national identity centred upon a set of traditions, laws and customs arising out of its Christian heritage'.[84]

It is a crutch on which Phillips regularly leans. 'Judaism and Christianity,' she writes, are 'the creeds that formed the bedrock of Western civilisation'.[85] Accordingly, what is so problematic about Muslim migrants, unlike their Jewish predecessors, is that they are 'foreign to the Judeo-Christian Western heritage'.[86]

Much is invested in this foundational Judeo-Christian heritage by anti-multiculturalists. The Australian Government makes special note of it in its information booklet for prospective citizens.[87] The Howard Government spruiked it regularly.[88] It is invoked as a historical anchor, yet the entire concept of a Judeo-Christian heritage, at least as used by Phillips to connote a harmoniously shared culture and values system, is a remarkable rewriting of history. The idea of that Jews and Christians share values or beliefs does not appear until probably the 1930s,[89] and the mere suggestion of it will have been anathema to many Christians until after World War II (the Jews, after all, were guilty of the most heinous of crimes: deicide). We forget that the attacks of militant Zionism against the British proceeded in part from Menachem Begin's belief in the incurable anti-Semitism of Christian Europe, including the British, whom he accused of 'determinedly shut[ting] their ears to the cry of Jewish blood dyeing the rivers of Europe' because they 'very eagerly wanted the Jews not to be saved'.[90]

In theological terms, the construction of a Judeo-Christian tradition is similarly incoherent.[91] Certainly, Jews and Christians partially share scripture. But they interpret it in fundamentally different ways, evidenced by the fact that no Jewish theologian could have imagined the Trinity. Indeed of the great monotheistic faiths, Christianity contributes the greatest theological departures. Islamic and Judaic monotheism have far more in common. Their legal traditions more closely converge. If there is an odd one out in this triumvirate, it is Christianity.

The forging of a Judeo-Christian tradition as a historical basis for Western civilisation is more a political act than a historical fact. Indeed the term's very creation was an attempt to resist the fascistic, anti-Semitic discourse of those who promoted the exclusively protestant identity of America.[92] To that end, it was a noble piece of linguistic innovation, quite at odds with the contemporary tendency to use it as a statement of exclusion.

This is how we create new cultures, new histories, new objects of veneration while pretending it was ever thus. Strange things can become artificially sanctified in the process. To return to two familiar reports by way of example, note how piggy banks became elevated to a 'time-honoured symbol of thriftiness'.[93] The effect is to convey a heightened sense of cultural assault, in spite of the fact that some banks had chosen to cease using them without violating national heritage regulations. Similarly were we introduced to 'the long-enshrined legal principle that taxis are a public conveyance open to all' so undermined in Minnesota.[94] Perhaps it really is a long-enshrined legal principle. We're unlikely to know because it is hardly a point of law that draws our regular admiration, or figures in our daily conversations. It is not the Magna Carta. But there is a message being conveyed in the gravity of the language here.

The Judeo-Christian example provides a neat illustration of how national narratives can change. The outcast, often brutalised Jew in time becomes the ontological insider. When Phillips speaks of a certain, stable British identity, her time horizons are vast: 'for around one thousand years, [Britain's] demographic profile remained remarkably stable,' she writes as though this implies an uncontested British identity.[95] It is a gloss that might have bemused many Welshmen and especially Scots over the centuries, who have quite clearly identified differently. Even (or especially) today, local identities are threatening to undermine the British union to the extent that the *Daily Telegraph* saw fit to launch a wonderfully blunt 'Call Yourself British' campaign.[96]

The simple fact is that nation-states are artificial creations often sustained by mythical narratives, coercion and violence.[97] Phillips writes as though they are divine truths, threatened by the immigration of those who, in the natural order, belong elsewhere. Here we have the nostalgic fiction of an ossified national culture that has ever been thus until multiculturalism and cultural relativism uprooted it. She assumes, indeed celebrates, a pre-existing monoculture. The main weakness of this portrait of course is that it fails to account for the fact that cultures are always contested and dynamic. Here we find the residue of the groupist mindset earlier identified. As minorities are essentialised, so too is the majority. Each belongs to a group with a distinct, unchanging culture. This leaves only one option for anti-multiculturalists: to ensure that minorities are pulled into line with their dominant hosts. There is no room for mutual evolution. One must yield to the other.

And yet Australia in particular is a compelling example of the fluidity of culture and identity. 'Anglo-Australian culture,' writes Levey, has 'been changed in various ways by successive waves of migrants, from the rise of soccer as a popular sport, to so-called 'new Australian cuisine', to the now national preference for coffee over tea and wine over beer'.[98] Such cultural accretions are an inevitable consequence of human interaction. Values and identity are similarly dynamic. This is, after all, a nation that once saw itself in thoroughly British terms, as a colonial outpost with a specific racial composition—that once denied its indigenous population a civic existence in accordance with this self-imagination. Human societies are inescapably responsive to their changing surroundings. Would Australian values now include environmentalism?

Naturally, this does not render culture entirely relative. Cultures differ, as anyone who has attempted to conduct business internationally can confirm. There are different boundaries of propriety, norms of formality, and yes, contrasting values systems. We should not be hesitant in acknowledging this. Moreover, it is true that Australia quite obviously has a predominantly British cultural inheritance. Our government follows the Westminster system.

Our courts are populated with barristers, not 'trial lawyers' or inquisitorial judges. We continue to play cricket.

Note, however, that these are only broad observations. Beyond this lies the rich terrain of dynamism and contestation—of culture and subculture, of current and countercurrent. Do not the value systems of artists regularly challenge those of the political elite? Have not the values of environmentalists long been at odds with those of big business, and if this is changing, is that not spectacular dynamism? Was not the Howard Government's WorkChoices policy an affront to the values of a significant portion of the electorate?

Such questions, and the associated arguments, could continue *ad infinitum*. We could unpack every value articulated in official government literature by assessing it in the light of government action if we wished. How is 'compassion for those in need' expressed in the policy of the mandatory detention of children? Was the invasion of Iraq a manifestation of our 'peacefulness'?[99] The problem with these questions is that in attempting to flesh out the meaning of Australian values, they simply end up articulating a contested political position. That is the nature of such intangibles. Any attempt at precise definition quickly becomes a subjective political orientation masquerading as a national consensus.

Conclusion

Folk devils are useful servants. At once they justify righteous rage and provide us the opportunity to articulate who we are through identifying who we are not. Predictably, more than any other minority in the post-September 11 era, Western Muslims have found themselves conscripted into this service. Whether it be through the discourse of politicians, or through media reporting and commentary, they have become the central protagonists in a refreshed rhetorical attack on multiculturalism throughout much of the Western world.

Those attacks are diverse, but in contemplating the most popular anti-multiculturalist narrative, we can observe the mythologies surrounding a moral panic in action. Obviously, much of this myth making concerns Muslims, and centres especially on the potentially disastrous threat they pose to an overly tolerant cultural majority. But equally important is the myth making concerning that majority.

'As a descriptor, multicultural fits nicely,' writes Albrechtsen on the basis that Australia has integrated millions of migrants. 'But once the 'ism' was added to multicultural, an accurate adjective morphed into a philosophy'.[100] And it is this 'philosophy' to which she objects. Yet when popular anti-multiculturalists take it upon themselves to defend Western values from multicultural assault, their account of Western culture is by no means merely descriptive. It is ideologically active in its own right, or in Albrechtsen's terms, philosophical. That is to say it promulgates no less an 'ism' than the one they construct as so culturally suicidal. This newly created 'ism' is not liberalism, for as we have seen, it strays too far into collectivist areas to be an untainted expression of liberal ideology. But consider the mythology that lies at the heart of popular anti-multiculturalist rhetoric: the remaking of history, the ossification of culture, and the attempt to reformulate one's political orientation as a statement of traditionally shared values. That can only properly be described as monoculturalism.

We live in an age of uncertainty. The monoculturalist's anxieties about postmodernism are neither accidental, nor entirely specious. In a world of rapid migration flows and instantaneous information flows, identities, values and cultures are subject to contestation and deconstruction with greater force than ever. The advent of terrorism in Western societies greatly exacerbates the sense of uncertainty. What was once thought to be solid is now fluid. But this is not the planned outcome of some corrosive ideological project of the left, as Phillips would have it. It is simply the inescapable logic of globalisation.

All this renders more urgent the project of reclaiming a sense of security and control, to impose order on the chaos. We might then expect essentialised worldviews—both religious and nationalist—to take up the challenge. Notes Catarina Kinvall:

> Hence, the strength of nationalism and religion as powerful identity-signifiers lies in their ability to convey unity, security, and inclusiveness in times of crisis. In conveying these beliefs they provide the idea of a 'home', a place where subjectivity can be anchored and securitised, giving both protection and safety from the stranger, the abject-other.[101]

Mythology is an inherent feature of this. In the pursuit of security, we must 'make claims to a monolithic and abstract identity'.[102] It is 'a process of establishing and confirming certain identity traits in yourself and the juxtaposition of these to others'.[103] That is the motor of monocultural essentialism, which 'means reducing self and other to a number of cultural characteristics [which] although constructed and fabricated, come to be seen as natural, unified features for describing the group'.[104]

This is a widespread phenomenon from which no society seems presently immune. Indeed, it would be quite possible to write this essay in the inverse: exploring Muslim monocultural discourses that trade on a mythical West and create a mythologised Muslim character in opposition to it.[105] It is evident in the rise of Hindu nationalism in India, Buddhist nationalism in Thailand or resurgent white nationalist politics across Europe. Here, perhaps, is the final lasting irony: that these groups that might otherwise despise one another share so much in the way of identity politics. They are cross-cultural analogues. Each reflects the other.

ON BEING MUSLIM AND AUSTRALIAN: REFLECTIONS FROM THE BADSHAHI MOSQUE

Shakira Hussein

SHAKIRA HUSSEIN

is undertaking a McKenzie postdoctoral fellowship on Muslim women, gender violence and racism at the National Centre for Excellence in Islamic Studies, University of Melbourne. She is a regular media contributor on issues including gender, multiculturalism, and Islam.

This was Ibrahim's gift to me: as we stood in the courtyard of Lahore's Badshahi Mosque, one of the glories of Mughal architecture, he swept his arm before us to encompass the domes and minarets, the cusped arches, the marble inlay and red sandstone, the tissue-paper kites fluttering in the smog-laden sky, and he said 'It's your Badshahi Masjid!'

And ever since I've felt that it really is mine, that I'm at home here, not a stranger in this place. Ibrahim lives in the crowded walled city, just beyond the mosque. The Badshahi has long been a refuge for him, and now it is a workplace. He knows the building intimately, not just its physical form but its life, its people, from the imam who leads the prayers to the boys who mind the shoes. He belongs here; I feel as though it is his to give.

Now Ibrahim and I are sitting in the courtyard of the mosque, discussing whether Ibrahim might ever become an Australian. Most Australians who have travelled to a developing country have had similar conversations: visas, job opportunities, sponsorship, can-you-help. But I take the conversation with Ibrahim more seriously than most such encounters. Ibrahim has all the qualities that successful immigrants of past generations have possessed. He is smart and quick witted, hard working and determined; he has the imagination and empathy necessary to understand people who are very different from him.

Unfortunately, these are not the qualities that immigration procedures are designed to assess. Pakistani youths with few formal qualifications are seldom considered deserving applicants for entry to Australia. And I have to confess to dark moments when I think that Australia does not deserve Ibrahim, his hopes and ambitions and dreams. In Pakistan, Ibrahim is Ibrahim, simply himself. In Australia, he would no longer be able to define himself. Instead he'll become a young Muslim male—as he is in Pakistan, too, of course, but in Australia this identity has taken on a new and threatening significance.

But then, Ibrahim is no stranger to hardship or to discrimination, which of course is why he wants to migrate. He is around nineteen years old, from a Panjabi village family that now lives in one small room in the walled city of Lahore. He is an only son with a mother and four younger sisters to care for. One son to four daughters is not a good ratio, not when all the girls will need expensive dowries if they are ever to be married. His mother and sisters work at home, assembling leather sandals as piecework. They never stop—except when they are performing other chores. Their hands are constantly stitching or weaving. The younger children play with the leather threads, and it is impossible to tell at what age this stops being play and becomes work. I've slept at their home, and whenever I stirred in the night, Ibrahim's mother and her eldest daughter were still working—silent, busy figures in the gloom—while the younger children slept piled together on the bare floor.

But Ibrahim is the male, the one who is supposed to be the main breadwinner. When I first met him, he worked at a machine in a neighbour's home, shaping small metal disks that were used to decorate wedding tents. These days, he earns his living guiding visitors around the Badshahi mosque. This pays better than working on the machine, but it is not a steady living. Few Western tourists visit Lahore these days, and the visitors from neighbouring countries and other parts of Pakistan do not pay so well. Ibrahim hopes that in Australia, he would be able to earn more money to provide for his family.

Ibrahim, then, would be an 'economic migrant', a term with neither the cachet of a 'skilled' or 'business' migrant, nor the heartstring tug of 'refugee'. Yet I cannot see him an unworthy migrant in terms of either motivation or potential. He is not a refugee, but his family's life is only ever one small mishap away from disaster. One of the little girls has died since I was last there—a short, undiagnosed illness, but I am sure that it was a disease of poverty. A toddler in my own extended Pakistani family network has died, too. Such deaths seem to happen so often, and with so little explanation. Children get sick, they are taken to the doctor, sometimes the medicine works and sometimes, well, sometimes it does not. To provide your family with a less precarious existence, to raise your own children in the expectation that they will survive into adulthood, is surely a legitimate aspiration.

And while it's true that Ibrahim would not bring much to Australia in terms of formal education or skills (let alone investment dollars), many of the most successful migrants brought as little, or less. They brought, instead, the shining possibility of building something new.

In Australia, I'm half Pakistani; in Pakistan, I'm half white. Many of my conversations in Pakistan are mirror images of the conversations I have in Australia. Australian Muslims find themselves endlessly required to 'explain' Islam to non-Muslim friends, colleagues, and even the most casual of acquaintances, trying to place the day's headlines into some kind of context. In Pakistan, it's Australia that I'm trying to contextualise. Both my Pakistani and Australian audiences tend to be sceptical of my attempts at transcultural dialogue. But 'explaining' contemporary Australia in Pakistan has helped to clarify my own thoughts, my sense of what it means to belong in Australia, and defend that sense of belonging.

The conversation with Ibrahim forces me to look ahead, to name my feelings about the future. The sense of uncertainty and insecurity among Muslims in Australia is so high that even some Australian-born Muslims with no sense of belonging anywhere else hesitate in making decisions such as buying a home or establishing a business—anything that cannot be quickly packed away and taken with you, 'just in case'. My sense of apprehension is less powerful, perhaps because I did not grow up with family memories of sudden and traumatic displacement. If you have already been forced from your home once, it is not hard to believe that it might happen again.

And even I feel the need to warn Ibrahim that these are not easy times to be Muslim in Australia. This does not come as news to him. Pakistanis are highly aware of discrimination and harassment experienced by Muslims living in the West, including Australia. I travelled to Pakistan in the immediate aftermath of September 11, contrary to dire warnings from the Department of Foreign Affairs and even more dire warnings from friends, who thought I was chasing a death wish. But no one in Lahore was in the least surprised to see me. People had heard about the firebombing of a Brisbane mosque, and they knew that Muslim asylum seekers were incarcerated in Australian desert prisons. They assumed that I had fled to the airport one step ahead of the Islamophobic mob, and, despite their trepidation for the future of their own society, they were horrified that I planned to return home. 'It's not safe for Muslims to live in the West anymore. Stay here and we'll find you a job in a posh girl's school.'

Stories circulated among middle-class Pakistanis about the experiences of friends and family living in the West: a cousin studying in London who was now too afraid to take public transport, an aunt who was wandering in an American shopping mall when a stranger grabbed her arm and twisted it hard, telling her, 'I just wanted you to know what pain feels like.' Some Pakistanis seemed to derive a certain perverse satisfaction out of these stories, as though Muslims living in the West were finally getting their comeuppance. Perhaps a few too many 'overseas Pakistanis' had returned home to boast a little too loudly about their suburban bungalows and new cars and children studying law or medicine at top universities. We had chosen the West, with its materialism, its wealth, its complacent assumption of superiority, and now, predictably, it had turned on us. Serve us right.

Yet still there is no shortage of young men like

Ibrahim who are keen to try their luck. I never knew my grandfather, but I imagine that he must once have been such a young man—a Panjabi villager who left his homeland for Singapore in the hope of building a better life for himself and for his wife and young son, my father. His descendents are now scattered across four continents, and most of them are like me 'half this and half that', as my aunt once disparagingly remarked. Half Anglo-Celtic Australian. Half Jewish. Half Irish Catholic. Half Sri Lankan Buddhist. So many long and complicated stories began the day my grandfather set out from his village. I wonder what complicated stories might be generated by Ibrahim's dreams: children and grandchildren who speak Urdu with an accent, or not at all, who know Lahore only through visits and family stories.

But that is all too far ahead. Ibrahim needs to know about now, about what it would be like for him in Australia, if by some stroke of good fortune he is able to secure a visa. And so I gather my wits and try to explain what it is like to be an Australian Muslim.

The first thing that needs to be said is that the phrase 'Australian Muslim', which now slides so easily off the tongue, came into circulation only fairly recently. Prior to September 11, Australian Muslims were visible not as Muslims but as Asians, or Lebanese, or Turks. That is not to say that they escaped hostile scrutiny. The 1996 federal election that swept the Howard government into office also saw the rise to political prominence of Pauline Hanson, who was disendorsed as a Liberal candidate after making provocative comments about Aborigines and welfare, but succeeded in being elected as an independent. Her maiden speech to parliament outlined her 'commonsense' opinions about issues such as the special privileges allegedly available to Aborigines and the danger that the country would be 'swamped' by Asians 'who have their own culture and religion, form ghettos, and do not assimilate'.[1] Hanson's inflammatory rhetoric was to provide an ugly soundtrack throughout the first two terms of the Howard government. While other politicians, including Howard himself, used dog-whistle politics to reclaim the electoral ground upon which Hanson had encroached, Hanson herself had no inhibitions about making her racialised dogma explicit.

A decade later, however, the focus of her attention had shifted. 'Asians' (who in Australian public discourse are generally those of East or South-East Asian descent) were no longer the primary threat to 'mainstream Australia'. Instead Hanson (who by this stage had long since left parliament and become a celebrity and figure of fun) called for a moratorium on Muslim immigration. 'People have a right to be very concerned about [Muslim migrants] because of the terrorist attacks that have happened throughout the world. I'm sick of these people coming out here and saying that our girls are like the meat market and the bible that is urinated on...am I supposed to be tolerant?'[2]

Hanson is not the only person to have shifted her opprobrium from Asians to Muslims in the years since September 11, 2001. While once conservative commentators illustrated the 'failure' of multiculturalism with reference to Cabramatta, triads and drug-dealing, they now speak of Lakemba (the heartland Sydney suburb for Lebanese Muslims), terrorism and culturally sanctioned gang-rape. Given the overlap between Asian and Muslim identity, in many cases it is the same individuals who are being targeted. For some Muslims, the post-September 11 fear mongering directed towards their religious identity is a continuation of the Hanson-era hysteria that targeted their ethnic identity. For others, however, it represents a radical disruption to their sense of belonging. While migrants from the Indian subcontinent may never have been considered mainstream Australians, they had not slotted into the common Australian usage of the word Asian, which tended to denote South-East Asian migrants and their descendents. Indo-Pakistanis tended to be skilled migrants with fluency in English, and so, until recently, had largely escaped the stigma that was attached to communities with less social and economic capital at their disposal. However, as commentators became more and more preoccupied with 'the Muslim problem', Muslims of all class, ethnic and sectarian backgrounds found themselves ascribed a common identity, and a common stigma.

And young men like Ibrahim—young Muslim men—have become particular folk-demons, haunting the Australian suburbs. Other young Muslim men have imprinted themselves on the collective psyche. Here are some of them: Mohamad Sidique Khan, Hasib Mir Hussain, Shehzad Tanweer and Germaine Lindsay. In the CCTV footage taken at Luton station, they're just a group of lads heading off for a day in London. They wear trainers and baseball caps like other young men of their age; they carry heavy backpacks with everything they'll need for their journey.

Of course, watching the footage, we know what none of those who saw the young men that morning could know—that this was not an ordinary morning, that these were not ordinary young men, that this day in London would come to be referred to as '7/7', that those young men would kill themselves and fifty-two others with the explosives concealed in their backpacks. The CCTV footage is haunting because it is so ordinary, and the apparent ordinariness of the London bombers—born and bred Britons, not exotic imports—is what makes them so terrifying.

Conversations about Muslims and Islam tend to refer to 'before' and 'after' September 11, but for Australian Muslims the attack that caused the most intense scrutiny was not September 11, nor the Bali bombings in which eighty-eight Australians died, but the bombings in London of 7 July 2005. This is partly because London is such familiar ground to many Australians, but even more because of the identity of the bombers themselves. The September 11 hijackers had lived in the USA as undercover agents, outsiders to the society they planned to attack. Most of those convicted of killing 191 people in the 2004 Madrid bombings were not Spanish. Before London, the threat was seen as reassuringly external, something that a vigilant government could hold at bay through 'border security'—a policy that the Howard government had zealously enforced even before September 11: the detention of men, women, and children in desert prisons for months and years at a time; the refusal to allow the *MV Tampa* to land after the ship had rescued 438 asylum-seekers from their sinking craft; the Pacific Solution, conceived in response to the Tampa affair, under which asylum seekers were bundled off to Nauru, apparently unfit to set foot on Australian soil even when confined to remote detention centres. This punitive approach was justified with rhetoric about 'queue-jumpers' and with manufactured stories about social undesirables who had thrown their children into the ocean in order to force the Australian navy to rescue them. In the the wake of the attacks on New York and Washington, then defence minister Peter Reith elaborated on this rationale by saying that a forceful response to asylum seekers was necessary to protect the lives of Australian citizens. 'Otherwise it can be a pipeline for terrorists to come in and use your country as a staging post for terrorist activities.'[3]

It does not seem particularly likely that terrorists would jeopardise complex and expensive operations by taking to the sea in flimsy vessels that were almost certain to be intercepted, if they managed to stay afloat for that long. Those desperate enough to risk their lives on such a voyage are infinitely more likely to be fleeing terror and violence than spreading it. The September 11 hijackers entered North America in comfort and safety and on regular visas. The fact that 'mainly Muslim asylum seekers' had entered the country through irregular channels made them improbable al-Qaeda operatives. Yet fencing them out of the country, or into internal detention centres, was portrayed as a national security imperative.

However, after the London bombings, the focus shifted from external threats to the enemy within: established Muslim communities within Australia. Suddenly, potential terrorists were not only aliens with strange accents and foreign passports. They could be native born, the boy next door, home grown. So it is not just Ibrahim himself who would be the object of fear in Australia, but his sons, who have not even been born—who are, at this point, entirely hypothetical.

The home-grown identity of the London bombers was as much of a shock to Australian Muslims as it was to anyone else. 'They were like us. Like me,' commented a friend, the French-born daughter of Maghrebi immigrants. This was an expression of mystification, not empathy. How could young men whose lives were like ours—who would have blended in unnoticed with the young men that we knew—have killed so coldly, so remorselessly, so many people, Muslim and non-Muslim, whose lives were also like our own?

That question has been subjected to endless analysis by police, media, politicians, bureaucrats and academics. An entire industry has been built around the question of why young men such as those who boarded the train to London that morning in July would commit indiscriminate murder. 'Unearthing the roots of Islamic extremism', identifying 'at risk' youths, debating whether their motives are political, socio-economic, or theological—these issues have become fodder for innumerable books, papers, symposiums, editorials and dinner-table debates. The search for common denominators among these murderous young men focused on one shared element: their Muslimness. And so other young Muslim men living in the West were similarly reduced to this common denominator, regarded as potential fifth columnists who carried within them a latent tendency to what the American commentator

Daniel Pipes referred to as 'Sudden Jihad Syndrome'. Those who succumb to Sudden Jihad Syndrome are not visibly disturbed or fanatical—they are regular people, normal-appearing Muslims, who inexplicably and unpredictably lurch into homicidal, religion-inspired rage. As Pipes notes, the supposed existence of Sudden Jihad Syndrome 'has the awful but legitimate consequence of casting suspicions on all Muslims. Who knows whence the next jihadi?'[4] Australian commentators such as John Stone similarly emphasised that all Muslims were to be regarded as suspect: 'we are now at war with international Islamist terrorism, and...therefore our Muslim community, collectively considered, now regrettably constitutes a potential threat'.[5]

Young Muslim men were to be feared not only as potential terrorists, but also as potential rapists. More names to associate with the phrase 'young Muslim men': Bilal and Mohammed Skaf. The K brothers. Names to evoke a shudder, a visceral twist of disgust. Their crimes proved as damaging to community relations as any terrorist attack.

Sydney in September 2000 was in party mode, all attention focused on the Olympics. With the city in an ebullient mood, police appeals for assistance over a series of gang rapes attracted little public attention. It was only later, when the offenders were identified as Australian-born Lebanese Muslim youths who had called one of their victims an 'Aussie pig' and told another that they were going to 'fuck [her] Leb style' that the media began to pay attention. The rapes were no longer a mundane crime story; in the eyes of many commentators, they were now the story of Muslim men committing racist hate crimes against Anglo-Celtic victims. The rape of 'our' women by 'their' men—there is no starker way of dividing 'us' from 'them'.

According to some of the media coverage, the rapes were not simply an attack on the young women concerned—they were an attack on Australia itself. Alan Jones believed that the rapes were an expression of 'contempt for Australia', while Miranda Devine referred to them as 'systemic ethnic cleansing by a group of men said to be of "Middle Eastern" extraction'.[6] But it was Janet Albrechtsen, writing in the *Australian*, who went to the greatest lengths to establish the link between the rapists' crimes and their Muslim identity. Albrechtsen claimed that the crimes committed by Bilal Skaf and his associates in Sydney were part of an international pattern, in which rapes committed upon 'young white girls' was a 'rite of passage' for some young Muslim men. However, as the ABC's *Media Watch* revealed, the research cited by Albrechtsen had made no association between the offenders' ethno-religious identity and their crimes. That particular detail was Albrechtsen's own invention.

Many Pakistani Australians distanced themselves from

the ugliness of the rapes and the ensuing public storm by reassuring themselves that the rapists were Lebanese, after all. The Lebanese men might be fellow Muslims, but they were low class types, trouble-makers and criminals. Their troubles had few implications for anyone else.

Then came the K brothers.

The K brothers (their full name was suppressed because one of them was underage at the time of the offences) were Pakistanis, Pashtuns from the North-West Frontier Province. They came to Sydney to live with their father, a doctor who had migrated some years earlier. Over a period of several months in 2002, the K brothers and a Nepali friend invited young women and girls to their home where they raped the girls, capturing their humiliation on camera.

The K brothers and their lawyers did everything possible to avoid guilty verdicts, prolonging the torment of their victims. The lawyers suggested that the victims had consented to sex, or had mistaken the identity of their attackers. One of the accused tried to bring about a mistrial by proclaiming to the courtroom that the brothers already had a previous conviction for rape, information that had been kept from the jury in order to ensure a fair trial. When they were finally found guilty, the lawyer for one of the brothers claimed in mitigation that his client's crimes were a result of his Pakistani cultural conditioning. The clash between his Pakistani upbringing and his new life in Australia had rendered K a 'cultural time bomb', who did not understand that women had the right to refuse to consent to sex.

The cultural time bomb claim brought a rare moment of agreement between the K brothers' defence team and media commentators such as Paul Sheehan, who had for the most part roundly condemned the brothers' attempts to evade responsibility for their crimes. Sheehan did not believe that the cultural defence should result in a lesser sentence, but he nonetheless found it an entirely plausible explanation for the rapes. The question, as Sheehan saw it, was how many more such time bombs there were ticking away in the Australian suburbs, waiting to detonate.

It is not hard to see why Australians would be alarmed at the idea of migrants introducing Pakistani gender norms to Australia. In Pakistan, discussions about sexual violence are dominated by the issue of the Hudood Ordinances, under which thousands of Pakistani women, including rape victims, have been jailed for adultery. Under the Laws of Evidence, a woman's testimony is worth less than a man's, so that if a case comes down to he says/she says, 'he says' always comes out ahead, and 'she' may be the one who ends up serving time. Most such women are eventually released, because the requirement for eyewitnesses makes it as difficult to prove adultery as it is to prove rape. But by that time, they may have spent years in detention.

But the Pakistani legal system's manifest inadequacy in dealing with sexual violence does not mean that Pakistanis regard rape as a trivial offence in which the issue of consent is irrelevant. The social sanction against rape is all the more powerful because the consequences for the victim are so serious. To rape a woman is understood as an attempt to destroy her entirely. It is understandable why the K brothers and their legal team should try to shift responsibility onto the young men's cultural conditioning; it is less explicable why media commentators should be so eager to concur.

But the language of tribalism had become an entrenched element of public discourse. In December 2005, this language metamorphosed into violence, as a crowd of around 5000 people gathered to 'reclaim' Cronulla beach from the young Lebanese Muslim men who had allegedly desecrated it by assaulting lifeguards and harassing women. The crowd was not overly selective about precisely which young Muslim men (and Muslim women) they assaulted. The point was to assert their 'Aussie pride'—and once again, it was young Muslim men who placed that pride at risk.

The next storm, however, was generated by an old Muslim man rather than a young one. In October 2006, the *Australian* reported on a sermon by Sheik Taj el-Din al-Hilali, the then Mufti of Australia. Hilali was commonly perceived as the spiritual leader of Australia's

Muslims, although his constituency was largely confined to Sydney's Lebanese community. Most Australian Muslims knew about Hilali only from media reports, and did not look to him for spiritual guidance. But when his sermon hit the headlines, we were all held responsible.

'If you take out uncovered meat and place it outside on the street, or in the garden or in the park, or in the back-yard without a cover, and the cats come and eat it...whose fault is it, the cats or the uncovered meat? The uncovered meat is the problem. If she was in her room, in her home, in her hijab, no problem would have occurred.'[7]

The Sheik's remarks would have created controversy at any time, but in the wake of the Sydney gang rapes, they created a firestorm. In one swift stroke, Hilali not only caused gross offence to women of all religious persuasions and none, he also gave new life to the allegation that young Muslim men pose a particular threat to Australian women. Just as it did not matter that non-Muslim men had also commited rape and harassed women on the beach, it did not matter that the Sheik's blame-the-victim mentality is broadly consistent with statements made by some Australian judges and lawyers over the years.

Reliable data on sexual violence is hard to come by, for obvious reasons. But all the available evidence indicates that offenders and victims are most often known to each other, members of the same tribe. This fact does not seem to have been taken on board either by Sheik Hilali or by commentators such as Sheehan and Albrechtsen, all of whom represent the rapist as a stranger. A Muslim rapist is most likely to rape a Muslim woman, just as an Anglo-Australian rapist is most likely to rape an Anglo-Australian woman, simply because rapists select their victims for their availability, for the likelihood that they will be shamed into silence. Contrary to Hilali's proclamation, hijab-wearing Muslim women have been raped in their own bedrooms, by men who had seen them without their hijabs because they were family members before whom there is no requirement to cover. And contrary to what one might believe after reading Albrechtsen or Sheehan, there is no empirical evidence whatsoever to suggest that Muslim men commit rape at a higher rate than do non-Muslims.

In the wake of Hilali's now infamous 'uncovered meat' sermon, I find myself thinking of all the late-night conversations I have ever had about rape. None of the women in these conversations was attacked from outside her own tribe. None reported her experience to the authorities. I remember one conversation in particular. My friend and I are sitting on the beach, in the dark, talking and talking. Our children are indistinct silhouettes some distance away. Every now and then one of them runs towards us, or away from us, and we either chase them away or call them back until they are in their permitted space: they must be close enough for us to watch them, but far enough away to be protected from the content of our conversation. We are in a place of utter darkness, my friend and I. Our children must not wander into it. My friend says 'I think this has happened to every woman. It's just that some women don't talk about it.'

I know empirically that this is not true. But as I reflect on how many similar conversations I have had, with Muslim and non-Muslim women alike, it often feels as though it is, as though rape is such a commonplace experience as to be almost universal, as though the world is full of walking wounded. Racialised public discussions of sexual violence are harmful not only because they perpetrate negative stereotypes about particular groups of men, but also because they focus only on the experiences of a particular type of victim, the woman whose attacker was the outsider, the stranger. One of them, not one of us. So many women carry the scars of sexual violence, and yet the most prominent public discussion of this issue in recent years has focused not on supporting women, but on stigmatising a particular group of men.

The men concerned, of course, have not responded passively. Some of them have entered into a weird symbiosis with the very media that has stigmatised them as terrorists and sexual predators. Young Muslim men are experiencing a profound sense of powerlessness in Australian society.

But the same media that has helped to produce this sense of powerlessness can also provide a salve, of sorts, if you are desperate enough to consider attention an adequate substitute for respect. Ours is a fame-seeking culture, after all. And young Muslim men can achieve front page headlines with one intemperate comment on an Islamic chat room. Their non-Muslim counterparts would have to pioneer an entirely new sexual technique live on reality TV to get that kind of attention. Some people discover that they don't like the spotlight as much as they thought they would, but of course, others thrive on it. The more outraged the editorials of the *Daily Telegraph*, the better.

And many of the young men have responded to disempowerment as young men so often do: by asserting their power over the nearest available target—the women in their lives. This has generated a legion of angry young Muslim women, who may not have generated the level of public attention bestowed upon their brothers, but whose anger is nonetheless burning white-hot. Trapped between dog-whistling media and politicians on the one side, and misogyny from elements in their own community on the other, Muslim women are highly conscious that speaking out against either source of oppression risks providing ammunition to the other. Far from empowering Muslim women, the stigmatising of Muslim men leaves women locked in silence. As angry as many

Muslim women are with particular Muslim men, all of them know other Muslim men who have earned their respect and their loyalty. Men like Ibrahim, for example, who sat with me in the courtyard of the Badshahi mosque, earnestly detailing his desire to become an Australian.

Of course, at this stage of his life, Ibrahim would be just as happy to become American, or British, or Swedish. But despite all that I have just described, I still hope that he might become Australian. As I have so often repeated to sceptical Pakistanis, it is not as though Australian Muslims encounter Islamophobic abuse every time they step outside the door. Australians in general seem to be far more tolerant than Australian public discourse would sometimes suggest. When Australian Muslims talk about negative experiences, they tend to focus on snide comments from politicians and media, rather than abuse experienced as they go about their everyday lives. Of course, the constant barrage of negative media has had its effect. Muslims—young Muslim men in particular—find themselves regarded with a certain wariness. But this wariness often gives way to trust, to understanding, to friendship.

The kites we watched floating over Lahore that day were theoretically banned, a ban that has been more sternly enforced since then. This is supposed to be for safety reasons—every year there are reports of people falling to their deaths while flying kites from the rooftop, or having their throats cut by the glass-coated kite strings used in kite-fighting tournaments. But kite flying has also been labelled 'unIslamic' by the Taliban and by Pakistani religious parties. And kite flying is not the only casualty, of course, as the violence spirals.

And so, back in Australia, I think that one day I would like to stand before the Opera House with Ibrahim, and sweep out my arm to encompass the harbour, the ferries, the bridge, the seagulls floating in the sky, and say to him 'It's your Sydney Opera House!' And I would like him to believe it, to feel that he is at home, and that his children will be at home here, too.

TESTING TIMES: CITIZENSHIP AND 'NATIONAL VALUES' IN BRITAIN AND AUSTRALIA

Graeme Davison

GRAEME DAVISON

is a Sir John Monash Distinguished Professor in the Department of History at Monash University. His books include *The Rise and Fall of Marvellous Melbourne*, *The Unforgiving Minute*, *The Use and Abuse of Australian History*, *Car Wars*, and, as co-editor, *The Oxford Companion to Australian History*. His current projects include a history of Monash University and a study of Australian nationalism.

'We are all nationalists now,' the British journalist Simon Jenkins observes.[1] He is reaffirming a now-familiar paradox: that as fast as globalisation dissolves the barriers between nations it strengthens moves to shore up the defences of the nation-state. New threats to the nation, including illegal immigration, ethnic and religious separatism, terrorism and the alienation of many citizens from formal politics, have combined to produce a new nationalist agenda.

In Europe, where these anxieties have become acute, social democrats as well as conservatives now appeal for a reinvigoration of 'national values'. Even nations once regarded as models of tolerance and internationalism have sought, under the pressure of immigration, especially from Islamic countries, to reinforce the allegiance of citizens and newcomers to national traditions. In Britain, former Prime Minister Gordon Brown made a series of speeches lamenting the loss of national identity and calling for educational and citizenship programs designed to inculcate 'Britishness'. In Denmark, school children must now demonstrate their knowledge of the canon of Danish literature. In Holland immigrants must attend 350 hours of classes on Dutch language and culture before qualifying for citizenship. And in France new citizens are examined on their understanding of the governing principles of the republic.[2]

The new nationalism has also produced an Australian echo. Among the last legacies of the Howard government was a program to reinvigorate the teaching of history in Australian schools and a compulsory test for new citizens designed to ensure their adherence to 'Australian values'. Introducing the *Citizenship Amendment Bill (2007)* the then Minister for Immigration, Kevin Andrews, summarised the imperatives behind the government's initiative:

> Australia can be proud of its history and have confidence in its future as one of the world's most stable democracies, where men and women are treated equally and the rule of law is paramount. A citizenship test will ensure a level of commitment to these values and way of life from all Australians, regardless of where they may originally come from.
>
> By having the knowledge and more importantly an appreciation of the events that have shaped this country and the institutions that have been

> established as a result will help foster a nation of people with a common purpose.[3]

A few months later, on the day he revealed his reasons for cancelling the visa of Mohammed Haneef, Andrews announced further measures to reinforce Australian values among prospective settlers to Australia. Applicants for a visa that could lead to permanent residence in Australia were obliged to sign a statement committing them to obey Australian laws and respect Australian values, while even those on temporary visas had to pledge to respect Australian values during their stay. 'In defending Western culture we should be unapologetic in requiring immigrants to make a commitment to our way of life,' the minister declared.[4] Even before they had experienced it for themselves, prospective residents in our country would be obliged to sign up to our way of life.

One of the features of the contemporary rhetoric of citizenship, a symptom of the shock and uncertainty unleashed by globalisation, is its pervasive dualism: the nation is characterised, alternately, as 'dynamic' and 'stable', 'diverse' yet 'cohesive'. Minister Andrews boasted of Australians' pride in their nation and in the stability of their democracy; yet implicit in his proposal, and in the subtext of his speech, was an anxiety that unnamed forces could sap that pride, dilute the nation's identity and endanger its stability.

The citizenship test polarised Australian opinion. Three-quarters of respondents to a Newspoll favoured the introduction of a test; yet most submissions to a Senate Committee opposed the bill.[5] Supporters cited the large numbers of younger Australians (300,000 according to one estimate) who were insufficiently conscious of their citizenship to bother registering as voters; but the test was not applied to most of them. Its introduction at a time of high immigration and fears of Islamic terrorism was almost certainly designed to allay the fears of old Australians as much as to smooth the integration of newcomers. Critics, including representatives of ethnic communities and academic advocates of multiculturalism, argued that the test was more likely to divide the community than to unite it. It assumed that anyone born in Australia would automatically subscribe to Australian values and applied the test only to newcomers, many of whom, it was argued, had demonstrated their love of freedom by their desire to come to Australia. Many in the ethnic community suspected that the purpose of the test was not to encourage newcomers to adopt Australian values but to intimidate or exclude those who were suspected of not sharing them.

The future of the citizenship test presented a dilemma for the Rudd Labor opposition. In May 2007, with a federal election in the offing, the Australian Labour Party supported the passage of the citizenship bill. Knowing that opinion polls supported a test, and unwilling to open itself to attack on patriotic grounds, Labor allowed the measure to go through without opposition. The only robust opposition to the bill came from the Liberal backbencher Petro Georgiou. Early in 2008, however, Labor's new Minister for Immigration Chris Evans released information showing that almost one-fifth of those taking the test were failing it, and the failure rate was especially high among applicants from Middle-Eastern and African backgrounds.[6] Many appeared to have failed because of their inadequate command of English as much as their poor understanding of the information in the textbook. The NSW Ethnic Communities Council immediately called for the test to be dumped, but the Minister rejected the appeal, affirming that the test would stay but initiated a review of it, concentrating on the content of the questions and the adequacy of support services for potential applicants.

The review, chaired by retired senior diplomat Richard Woolcott, was a pragmatic exercise, designed to ease ethnic sensitivities and raise the pass rate without calling into question the principle of the test. It recommended a modification of the standard of English required of new citizens and simplified the form and content of the test. Many submissions to the review had included complaints of the irrelevance of the historical information applicants were required to memorise. Why was it important for new citizens to know about the Australian cricketer Don Bradman, for example? Woolcott proposed to purge the test of historical trivia ('Don Bradman dismissed', one headline read),[7] and refocused it on the principles underlying the central act of becoming a citizen, the Pledge of Commitment:

> From this time forward, [under God] I pledge my loyalty to Australia and its people, whose democratic beliefs I share, whose rights and liberties I respect, and whose laws I will uphold and obey.[8]

Rather than a trivial pursuit quiz on Australian history, the test would become a kind of civic catechism on democratic principles such as respect for the worth of the individual, freedom of speech, religion, and association, equality of the sexes, tolerance and peacefulness.[9] New citizens would be encouraged 'to understand how Australia developed from its uncertain beginnings as a British colony to the stable and successful multicultural nation it is today.' The information about Australian history, customs, national days, flags, sporting and other heroes was now relegated to a second section of the citizenship textbook which applicants were invited to read but on which they were not obliged to be tested.

By retaining the citizenship test, the Australian Labor Party followed in the path of the British Labour Party, which had previously introduced a similar test designed to inculcate 'British values'. During 2006–07, when I frequently travelled back and forth between Melbourne and London, I became increasingly aware of the interesting resonances and dissonances between the British and Australian debates on citizenship. The social and political circumstances of the two countries were not congruent in every way, but it was clear that each was wrestling with similar dilemmas, and—in Australia's case at any rate—responding to ideas and policies generated by the other.

Gordon Brown, as both Chancellor and Prime Minister, placed the promotion of 'British values' at the centre of his vision for a progressive, cohesive, multicultural Britain. Brown was worried, with more reason than Australian politicians, about the alienation of young Britons from civic engagement and political participation and by the rise of Islamic extremism, although his concern with issues of citizenship long predated the London bombings and other terrorist outrages. He supported citizenship tests, but regarded them as only part of a more ambitious program designed to reinforce values of freedom, responsibility and fairness as the foundation of a more cohesive Britain. In an address to a conference on 'Britishness' at the Commonwealth Club in January 2007, he expanded on this theme:

> British citizenship is about more than a test, more than a ceremony—it is a kind of contract between the

> citizen and the country, involving rights and responsibilities that will protect and enhance the British way of life.
>
> Citizenship means there are common rules and accepted standards. There is now agreement with the proposition I made some time ago that for new citizens, learning English should be a requirement. New citizens should have an understanding of our history and our culture.[10]

Like Kevin Andrews, Brown stressed 'common values', 'common rules and accepted standards', responsibilities as well as rights, and the importance of a knowledge of history and culture to an understanding of citizenship. But he went well beyond Andrews in his suggestion that applicants for citizenship should undertake some form of community service before enjoying the rights of citizens. His definition of British values was more egalitarian and pluralist than Andrews' definition of Australian values. In a speech to the British Fabian Society, he invoked George Orwell's complaint that the left too often surrendered the claims of patriotism to the right. Rather than an inward-looking, xenophobic, reactionary and defensive patriotism, 'Britishness', Brown argued, embraced progressive traditions of 'liberty for all, responsibility by all, fairness for all'.[11]

Early in 2008 a committee chaired by Lord Goldsmith

QC conducted a wide-ranging review of citizenship issues in the United Kingdom.[12] A study commissioned by the inquiry from the Oxford sociologist Anthony Field confirmed some of the fears underlying Brown's rhetoric. Identification with 'Britain' was declining compared with identification with its constituent parts, England, Scotland and Wales. As many as 20 per cent of Britons, especially young people and members of black African and Caribbean communities, though significantly *not* South Asian communities, had strong negative feelings towards the nation. In Britain as in Australia, many applicants for citizenship failed the test (over 40 per cent from the Bangladeshi community) and it was widely perceived as an exercise in mere rote learning. Goldsmith proposed major amendments of British citizenship law, especially to reinforce the link between permanent residence and citizenship.[13] While retaining the test as one avenue to citizenship, he also recommended major reforms to mandate citizenship education in schools and to create new rituals of citizenship, including citizenship ceremonies and a national day modelled on Australia Day. Community service could be considered as a part of citizenship education but only on a voluntary basis.

Over the past five years, governments in Britain and Australia have each introduced, reviewed and modified the process by which newcomers are inducted into citizenship. The circumstances provoking the reviews, notably the large numbers of applicants failing the citizenship test, were similar, but the outcomes in each country were quite different. While Australia moved to relax the test requirements in the interests of social inclusion, Britain sought to embed the test more firmly in civic attitudes and behaviour and to strengthen its symbolic importance. In each country, it seems, attitudes to the citizenship test have become a kind of litmus test of national morale in the face of threats, real or imaginary, to its integrity. Who is the test designed to reassure? And what are the prospects of it achieving its purpose? Does it simply test the recall of rote-learned facts? Or does it act as an effective filter, assuring nationals that new citizens really have absorbed its core political values?

The demand for citizenship tests and values statements is a symptom of an unresolved tension in our political culture. As governments of all persuasions have become committed to neo-liberal doctrines of freedom and deregulation, they have left many of their followers uneasy about the vacuum created by the abandonment of unifying ideals, what conservatives associated with 'social order' and social democrats with 'community'. As the process of economic liberalisation has unfolded, stripping bare all impediments to the free play of the market, marginalising trade unions, voluntary associations, churches and other agencies of social protection, society threatens to dissolve into a congeries of disconnected individuals. As the state does less for people, it is perhaps not surprising that people want to do less for the state. The fabric of community institutions through which people learned to practise democratic values becomes attenuated. People increasingly retreat into the private sphere of the household and family, withdraw from civic and political engagement, and withhold their trust from politicians who are seen, however unfairly, as remote and self-seeking. While Australians are proud of their country—possibly prouder than the peoples of any other nation, going by international polls—they have a weak sense of citizenship as measured by their cynical and detached attitude towards politicians and political life in general.[14]

What are the common values that enable citizens to live together in harmony? If Australians answered that question a century ago, they had ready-made answers. Australia was British, white, Christian and constitutional-monarchist. Some Australians, especially those of Irish heritage, would have objected to some, though not all, of those values; but with the exception of a short period during and after World War One, their dissent did not imperil the national consensus. Now most of those traditional pillars of national identity have crumbled. We are no longer universally British, white or Christian and we remain monarchist in only a vestigial sense. Democrats will point to a core of generic liberal democratic rights: free speech, respect for the law, equality of the sexes, freedom from racial or ethnic discrimination, freedom from arbitrary arrest and imprisonment, etc. These rights are a precious possession, and their observance is not to be taken for granted, even within the so-called democratic countries of the West. But are they enough? Does a mutual recognition of individual liberties and differences provide an adequate foundation for a cohesive society?

There are important differences of tone and emphasis between the British and Australia approaches to national values and citizenship, and between the political and social contexts from which they emerge. In Britain, where the sense of national selfhood was once more confident, and the pressures of separatism and social fragmentation are now greater than in Australia, the appeal to reassert national values has a more urgent undertone. The home-grown terrorism revealed by the London bombings has only added to the sense of national disintegration already generated by Scottish and Welsh devolution, and by the fear of many Britons that they are being absorbed in the European community. Australians have long been used to contrasting their own immature sense of national selfhood with the deeply rooted traditions of their former motherland. While we might not yet be sure who we are, at least, we thought, the British knew who they were. But now, it often seems, it is the British who are unsure of their identity, while Australians have become, to borrow a phrase, more relaxed and comfortable.

The national values that patriots now seek to reinforce are seldom uniquely British or Australian, although they may seek to clothe them in a local vernacular. So Australian politicians speak of mateship, not fraternity; the fair go, not egalitarianism. Yet under the local labels, the values they are proclaiming are essentially those of Western liberal democracy. Britain, the country where parliamentary government first emerged, may have a special claim to regard these values as its own, but the point of calling them 'British' or 'Australian' is not to acknowledge their historical origins. What drives the new nationalists is the apparent fraying of the link between national identity and citizenship. By invoking national values, they are seeking not so much to put a ring around everything that is essentially Australian or British as to exclude from the ring those values that are '*un*-Australian' or '*un*-British', especially those that are in conflict with liberal democracy.

Some of what are now defined as national values, such as the equality of the sexes, would not have been regarded as quintessentially British or Australian half a century ago. Meanwhile, there are sentiments and values with a claim to be regarded as British or Australian—such as a love of one's countryside, or of a national game, pride in the achievements of one's countrymen or women, a desire to wave the Cross of St George or the boxing kangaroo—that are only tenuously connected to citizenship. Until recently, applicants for Australian citizenship faced questions about Australian fauna and flora, as well as Australian heroes and political history, but, as the Woolcott review discerned, it is harder to deny citizenship to someone who can't recognise a gum tree or a koala than to someone who can't speak English and doesn't know how to vote.

In its renewed emphasis upon civic duties and responsibilities, and on the values that underlie them, the new nationalism clashes with the more contingent and pluralist understandings of national selfhood that have become almost standard in Australia and Britain over the past three or four decades. One symptom of this tension has been the way in which recent debate has veered between the concepts of 'national values', 'way of life' and 'national identity'. 'National values', like the old-fashioned idea of 'national character', is an essentially ethical and unitary concept. It affords an apparently more solid foundation for national selfhood than the more contingent and malleable idea of 'identity'.[15]

The call to reinforce national values has been accompanied by a new emphasis on the teaching of a unified, factual, narrative version of the nation's past. Early in 2006, in the aftermath of the London bombings, Chancellor Gordon Brown addressed this plea to the British Fabian Society:

> British history should be given much more prominence in the curriculum—not just dates, places and names, nor just a set of unconnected facts, but a narrative that encompasses our history. And because citizenship is still taught too much in isolation, I suggest in the current review of the curriculum that we look at how we root the teaching of citizenship more closely in history.

Two weeks later, on Australia Day, John Howard made an almost identical plea, contrasting his desire for a unifying narrative of the national past with the 'mushy relativism' of academic history. Lord Goldsmith has also called for 'a narrative, non-legalistic statement of the rights and responsibilities of citizenship; and a national day...which would provide an annual focus for our national narrative.'[16]

The prominence of the word 'narrative' in the political rhetoric of nationalism was an interesting symptom of unease. It suggested that the power of history to unite the nation is only as great as the coherence of the story told about it. What nationalists seek is not an open-ended investigation of the past but a set of core beliefs about it. They are looking not for boats to explore the world, but for anchors to stay citizens against currents that might otherwise carry them away.

Many historians will not know whether to feel more flattered or troubled by the confidence politicians now place in narrative history as a force for social cohesion. We would all like to see history restored to a more prominent place in the school curriculum, but none of us, surely, is naïve enough to suppose that compulsory history lessons, or rote knowledge of a few facts of Australian history, will prevent disenchanted or alienated youths from committing terrorist acts, or even get them to vote. Only the gradual erosion of more traditional pillars of national selfhood can account for the exaggerated confidence that politicians now invest in history as a binding force. What Australians are now supposed to have in common is not shared ethnic or homeland origins, or even a set of shared political values, but a shared story.

Does Australia actually have such an agreed narrative? In the course of the nineteenth century, Australian nationalists, drawing inspiration from their American, Canadian and South African counterparts, fashioned narratives of conquest and settlement, of emancipation and deliverance, of law-giving and state-making and of reconciliation.[17] Each has influenced the telling of our national story; yet each is in some way either compromised or incomplete. The story of conquest and settlement is compromised by the dispossession and murder of the first people, the

Aborigines. Without a moment of revolutionary change, the story of our political emancipation is incomplete. Our constitutional history evokes nothing as glorious as the making of the American constitution. And unlike our nearest European neighbour, New Zealand, we made no historic compact or treaty to legitimise or repair our first transgression. Only one master narrative, our *Odyssey,* the story of Anzac, seems to unite us all, and then only because it has been purged of many of the elements that once divided us.

In the broad debate that is now underway in Europe as well as in Australia, I detect three broad positions I will call, for simplicity's sake, the conservative, liberal-pluralist, and civic republican positions.

Conservatives have a deep attachment to ideas of political or religious authority. They fear that without guidance from above people are in danger of succumbing to false beliefs and that society will collapse into warring tribes. That many contemporary social conservatives are also economic liberals only increases their anxiety. They are hostile to multiculturalism because they fear that it erodes the necessary 'core' of belief without which society will disintegrate. Once that core would have been found in Christianity or the Judaeo-Christian tradition. The decline of organised religion in the West, however, only accentuates its sense of vulnerability to the resurgence of other faiths, like Islam.[18] The conservatives now seek to ground their beliefs in a 'core' of 'unifying' and 'overarching' (the adjectives are their own) 'national values', derived, not from a religious creed, but from the history of the nation. The history they seek is one simultaneously factual (hence their hostility to anything that smacks of postmodernism and relativism) and purposive, that is, structured as a teleological narrative, an epistemological conundrum explicable only by the essentially political imperatives that shape it. The philosopher David Conway, a leading member of the British think-tank Civitas captured the essence of the conservative approach when he called for the abandonment of programs of citizenship education and the reinstatement of British history taught, explicitly, in the manner of the great Whig historians, as a narrative of the unique unfolding of the principles of British liberty.[19] One of the reasons for the bitterness of the so-called 'history wars' in Australia has been the reluctance of most academic historians not simply to subscribe to the government's 'core' of national values, but to regard history as a journey towards a preordained destination.

The liberal-pluralists, a group that includes a good proportion of the objectors to the citizenship test, and most of the so-called 'ethnic lobby', give relatively little weight to questions of social cohesion and civic responsibility.[20] Their primary interest is in advancing the case of ethnic or religious sub-groups for self-expression and recognition. They argue, with some reason, that citizenship tests may do more to exclude than to integrate the groups being tested. The world, they suggest, is now too small to be concerned with narrow questions of nationality or ethnicity. We must move beyond nationalism towards an internationalism or cosmopolitanism that recognises the essential plurality of cultures.[21] Beyond a guarantee of a broad and universal bill of human rights, the state should make as few demands as possible on the lives of citizens. Civic values, they imply, are acquired by osmosis and, if they are not, nobody should be too worried; a pluralist society can survive quite happily as 'a community of communities' based on a mutual recognition of differences. For the most part, liberal pluralists see little need for citizenship tests, history education or other nation-building exercises. Their understanding of national history, after all, is an optimistic one: that, while each generation of newcomers may experience some hostility, in the long run they are accepted and integrated. This optimistic reading accords reasonably well with Australian experience, though less convincingly with recent British experience. As a people, we Australians are traditionally reluctant to interfere with the beliefs and practices of others as long as they don't interfere with ours. In morals, if not in economics, we are laissez-faire. High living standards and spacious suburbs have reinforced that outlook. But perhaps the pluralists take social cohesion too much for granted. Can we afford to assume that the process of benign neglect will continue to integrate newcomers into Australian society? Or does the need for social cohesion place more definite obligations on both new and old Australians to learn and exercise their civic responsibilities?

In response to these questions, some British and Canadian thinkers have attempted to define approaches to questions of citizenship that avoid the shortcomings of both the conservative-authoritarian and the liberal-pluralist positions.[22] Common to many of these writers is the republican idea of participatory democracy. While the citizens of such an ethnically and religiously diverse nation may have a range of overlapping ethnic, religious, sexual and other identities, they are joined through their common participation in the affairs of the nation. This sense of common citizenship not only supports traditional patriotism but also such social democratic projects as a national health service.[23] Multiculturalism, according to this perspective, gives each group a place at the table and a right to argue its case, but not an unqualified right for its demands to be met.[24] Groups that do not recognise the state, or are fundamentally hostile to it, effectively exclude themselves from this national conversation, and if the state discourages the formation of such groups, their members cannot regard themselves as being unfairly discriminated against.

In Australia, similar arguments have been advanced by Tim Soutphommasane in his recent book *Reclaiming Patriotism: Nation Building for Australian Progressives*, which applies some of the lessons of the British debates on citizenship to Australian circumstances. Love of country, Soutphommasane argues, is a popular sentiment that the Left ignores at its peril. Under Howard, national sentiment was ruthlessly exploited, not only to marginalise Muslims and other minorities, but to divide his political opponents. Political pragmatism, as well as democratic principle, dictates that progressives embrace a patriotism that is outward-looking and inclusive rather than inward-looking and discriminatory. Australian national values, such as fairness, equality and mateship, are not uniquely Australian but take on the colour of our own historical experience.[25]

Such a republican conception of political life rests upon liberal-democratic conventions and traditions not necessarily shared by all citizens, old or new. Civic republicans have often emerged as strong advocates of citizenship education designed to inculcate a basic knowledge of these conventions and traditions. The political scientist Bernard Crick, biographer of George Orwell, headed the 1998 commission that led to the introduction of the British citizenship test. Crick favours citizenship education with what he calls 'a light touch'. Rather than attempting to indoctrinate would-be citizens with correct values, or a single unified narrative of the national past, citizenship education, he argues, should focus mainly on practical matters designed to enable newcomers to enter the mainstream of British life where, he believes, the real work of social and political acculturation takes place.[26] So applicants for citizenship in the United Kingdom are asked questions about how to apply for social welfare benefits, what services they can expect from the National Health Service, how the voting system works. Some of the objectors to an Australian citizenship test consider that it is demeaning to control access to the high obligations of citizenship through something that looks like a driver's license test. Yet a kind of driver's test—a practical and non-ideological examination designed to equip citizens to claim their rights and exercise their civic responsibilities—may be much less objectionable than a test that purports to measure the applicants' adherence to an inevitably contentious definition of 'national values'.

The study of history, as an open-ended critical inquiry into the national past, has an important part to play in such a process of citizenship education. By interpreting the inherited political landscape, stimulating critical reflection on national institutions and policies, and modelling the processes of democratic decision-making, history is an indispensable aspect of citizenship. Engaging students or prospective citizens in active reflection on the national past in ways that recognise its plural and contingent character may, paradoxically, do more to incorporate prospective citizens into the political nation than forced compliance with an official version of the national story. As Anna Clark discovered in her conversations with Australian teachers and students, historical literacy is better acquired by challenging students to 'do' and 'make' history than by testing their recall of prescribed knowledge.[27] Realists may object, saying that before newcomers can practise that more active, critical citizenship, they must first acquire, more or less by rote, a working knowledge of the nation's history, political institutions and values. There is an element of truth in this, but care must be taken not to treat adult applicants for citizenship as children, unversed in political thinking and incapable of active learning.

Applicants for British citizenship prepare for their examination by reading a book entitled *Life in the United Kingdom*. It is a sensible, informative, non-partisan sourcebook of information on all aspects of British life. The most recent edition of the book gives rather more attention to history and tradition than previous editions. It begins with a brief chronological overview of British history and continues with sections on society, government, everyday needs, employment and the law. It concludes with a section on 'Building Better Communities' stressing the importance of 'shared values', respect for the law, and getting on with one's neighbours, though without saying much about what those shared values are. 'Knowing about these things will make it easier to become a full and active citizen', it concludes, 'but reading a book is no substitute for being part of society'.[28]

The evolution of the Australian citizenship test followed a rather different path from the British one. The Howard government published its own textbook for prospective citizens: *Life in Australia*. As the title suggests, it bore a superficial resemblance to its British counterpart, partly perhaps because the same consultants designed the architecture of the multiple-choice test used in both countries. It also contained sections on social customs (queuing, saying please and thankyou, the Australian preference for the use of first names), common expressions ('no worries', 'bring a plate' and BYO) and guides newcomers to social services, schools and other state agencies in a similarly neutral, helpful way. But the content and emphases of the two books were very different. *Life in Australia* was shaped, from its opening paragraphs, by an emphasis on 'Australian values'.

> Australian values include respect for the equal worth, dignity and freedom of the individual, freedom of speech, freedom of religion and secular government, freedom of association, support for parliamentary

> democracy and the rule of law, equality under the law, equality of men and women, equality of opportunity and peacefulness. These also include a spirit of egalitarianism that embraces fair play, mutual respect, tolerance, compassion for those in need and pursuit of the public good.[29]

I wonder if it is just clumsy drafting that makes the social values announced in the second and shorter sentence (fair play, compassion, etc.) sound as though they are subordinate to the individualist values (freedom of the individual, freedom of speech, etc.) expressed in the first?

At first sight, there was little in this summary of Australian values that anyone could reasonably gainsay. To be sure, these were not uniquely Australian values but shared, as the book admits, by many other countries, 'to some extent'. Only as the principles were expounded in the rest of the book did its target—the stereotype of Islamic extremism—come clearly into view. The freedom and dignity of the individual, we are told, proscribes 'the use of violence, intimidation or humiliation as a means of settling conflict in our society'. While Australians uphold freedom of speech, prospective Australian citizens are also reminded of laws against 'inciting hatred against others because of their culture, ethnicity or background'. Australia has a secular government, so 'religious laws have no legal status in Australia'. Mateship means that neighbours 'help each other in the event of trouble and report anything unusual or suspicious to the local police station'. (The old Australian words 'dobber' and 'scab' did not appear in the textbook's glossary of Australian terms.) Australia valued cultural diversity, 'but nonetheless all religious and cultural practices must conform to Australian laws. For example state and territory laws prohibit practices involving genital mutilation and violence in the home.'

Particularly troubling, and not just to Muslims, was the contention that 'Australian values' must prevail over all others: 'All Australians,' the textbook said, 'are asked to make an *overriding* commitment to Australia, its laws, its values and its people.' Many Christians and Jews, as well as Muslims, would regard loyalty to country as secondary to their allegiance to God. The makers of the United States and Australian constitutions believed that the nation was constituted 'under God'. In his persuasive defence of multiculturalism, the philosopher (Lord) Bhikhu Parekh argues that:

> Citizenship represents one of the individual's several identities, and does not automatically trump all others. As human beings we have moral obligations to people outside our political community, and these may modify, limit and in exceptional circumstances override [that word again!] our obligations as citizens. Although political obligations generally

> override ethnic and religious obligations, this is not always the case. If the state were to require me to betray my parents and friends, spy on or malign my ethnic or religious community, or convert to another religion, I would find its demands unacceptable.[30]

Not only Muslims but also many Christians and Jews would concur. Politicians are especially prone to the assumption that civic obligations override all others, but in imposing that assumption on others, who may not share it, they risk alienating some otherwise good prospective citizens. You don't have to require citizens to give the nation an overriding loyalty unless you already suspect that their adherence to their faith or family is incompatible with it.

The Howard citizenship test was like a mass immunisation program, to which all prospective citizens must submit, even though only some were suspected of being susceptible to the disease. At first sight, *Life in Australia* was an invitation to newcomers to accept the rights and responsibilities of citizenship; implicitly, it served notice that some prospective citizens, notably some Muslims, may have to renounce values that are inconsistent with Australia's. In November 2007, a new edition of the book, retitled *Becoming an Australian Citizen*, appeared. It omitted several of the most invidious allusions, for example those to police stations and genital mutilation cited above, but the underlying rationale of the text remained.

In 2010, *Becoming an Australian Citizen* was consigned to the dustbin of official history in favour of a new 'test resource book', *Australian Citizenship: Our Common Bond*, embodying the recommendations of the Woolcott review. The new book subtly tilts the balance away from the Howard government's vision of a nation united around common values towards a more inclusive idea of nationhood. 'Australia has become a multicultural society of harmony and acceptance. It is a country where migrants, Indigenous people and others born in Australia can feel free to pursue their goals in peace. It is a place where past conflicts and resentments can be left far behind.'[31] The first 'testable' section of the book falls into three parts: a brief overview of 'Australia and its people', summarising the nation's history, geography, national days, flags and anthem; a longer outline of its 'democratic beliefs, rights and liberties'; and a formal description of 'government and the law in Australia'. The core of testable civic information has been carefully winnowed from the husk of 'irrelevant' facts about the nation's geography, heroes, folk traditions and, most conspicuously, from a narrative of 'Our National Story', all of which are relegated to the 'non-testable' second section of the book. The hope, presumably, is that new citizens will absorb something of the more colourful material in the second section while they get down to memorising the drier, more didactic, core knowledge in the first. And nowhere is it implied: 'Muslims please take note.'

In slimming down the citizenship test, the Woolcott review hoped to make it easier for newcomers to become citizens. A kind of political catechism, it is designed to ensure that new citizens understand, in a basic way, what they are promising. Yet the test is not just educational—'to provide an opportunity for individuals to learn about the responsibilities and privileges of citizenship'—since the state could obviously provide an opportunity to learn without requiring new citizens to show what they had learned.[32] Rather, as the committee also recognised, it is designed 'to provide *assurance to the wider community* that prospective citizens understood the concepts in the pledge to which they were committing'.[33] It is not just for the benefit of the new citizen; it is part of an implied contract between the new citizen and the political community.

The citizenship test is not just an educational device; it is also a rite of passage marking the induction of the stranger into the national community. In his famous analysis of rites of passage, the anthropologist Arnold van Gennep stressed their sacred or magical character. In traditional societies, these rites were often accompanied by trials of pain and stamina, processes of purification, times for introspection and reflection, the telling of sacred stories and the use of symbolic representations. Many of these features of a rite of passage are present, thinly veiled, in discussions of the citizenship test, pledge and ceremony. In stressing national values as the basis for the citizenship test, national leaders seek not just to ensure that the new citizens have absorbed certain information and that they understand the social contract they are making but that they have acquired some of the outlook and traditions of the community they are entering.

In reducing the core of 'testable' knowledge to the principles of the pledge, the new Australian citizenship test aims to be more inclusive. But by retaining a supplement of non-testable information on the history which produced those principles, the heroes who fought for them, and the folkways which illustrate their everyday use, it also attempts to keep faith with those nationals who would like new citizens to share rather more of their own sense of what it means to be Australian. In becoming an Australian, they may argue, newcomers pledge allegiance to a country with its own distinctive traditions and way of life, not just a set of abstract principles. 'To speak of being attached to one's laws, even if they are derivative of liberty, seems a sterile sentiment', Tim Soutphommasane observes.[34] But is it possible for new citizens to acquire, under the pressure of a compulsory test, anything like the deeper sense of belonging that older Australians may feel? Many of them come with their own keen appreciation of the benefits of democracy, born of experience in more oppressive lands. All that the rest of us can fairly require of new citizens is a commitment to the country and its governing principles; not the mature understanding and sense of attachment that comes with the years.

Even in its revised form, the Australian citizenship test continues to rankle with many prospective citizens. One of the most persistent criticisms is of its inherent unfairness.[35] While it may be reasonable to require new citizens to undergo some rite of passage, many of the arguments for a test apply just as well to native-born Australian citizens who are just as ignorant of their rights and responsibilities. 'There are people who have been living in Australia all their lives and don't know the answers to most of these questions', one applicant observed. Many Australian citizens, including relatives of applicants, admitted to flunking the trial questions. Most objectors thought this was a good enough reason to dispense with the test altogether, although some proposed to make it fair by requiring other Australians to take it too. 'I think *all* citizens should sit this—including Australians born here', one insisted.

According to the citizenship textbook, the fair go is a keystone of Australian democracy; so imposing the test on newcomers while exempting locals seems to contravene the very democratic principles the test aimed to teach. It would be a brave Australian government, however, that obliged

Australian-born citizens take the test, especially if failure meant that they could lose their national birthright. The brutal truth is that natives inherit rights that newcomers must earn. 'Why would Australians need to know the answers [to the test]?', one realist bluntly inquired. 'It's their country! They didn't *choose* to become Australians. People who *choose* Australia as a place to live should not complain that they have to know things that the locals don't know.'

Even so, if citizenship really is a 'common bond', there could surely be more reciprocity in how it is promoted and practised among all Australians. In Britain, Lord Goldsmith proposed that the citizenship test for newcomers should be accompanied by a more extensive program of citizenship education for British schoolchildren, and that new citizens, both natives and immigrants, should take part in the proposed new citizenship ceremonies. By stressing the common bond between citizens, rather than the special obligations of newcomers to conform to a code of 'national values', these measures would not only remove a source of irritation but also give symbolic expression to a sense of common citizenship. If the citizenship test cannot be reformed to reflect such a more inclusive and reciprocal understanding of citizenship, it may be better to dispense with it altogether.

Citizenship education, after all, plays only a small part

in creating a cohesive society. The recent enthusiasm for citizenship tests in Britain and Australia is perhaps more symptomatic of the anxieties of the official class, and of their need to demonstrate to the electorate that they are tough on terrorism and vigilant in defending national borders, than an effective means of inculcating good citizenship. We should be wary lest, in attempting to draw newcomers into the political community, we impose conditions that tend to push them out. Unless we also follow immigration, employment, housing, educational and health policies that reflect a commitment to social inclusion and equal opportunity then asking new citizens to give lip service to national values or democratic principles will only compound their marginalisation. It is as important for old citizens to live up to national ideals as it is for newcomers to know and share them.

MULTICULTURALISM AND THE UNGOVERNABLE MUSLIM

Ghassan Hage

GHASSAN HAGE

is Future Generation Professor of Anthropology and Social Theory at the University of Melbourne. He has written extensively on multiculturalism, nationalism, racism and migration in a comparative perspective. His books include *Home/World*, *White Nation*, *Against Paranoid Nationalism*, *Arab Australians* (ed.) and *Waiting* (ed.).

Marx's famous polemically intended formula 'The hand-mill gives you society with the feudal lord; the steam-mill, society with the industrial capitalist' is often seen as exemplifying what has become known as technological determinism: the view that society is the simple outgrowth of particular technological innovations. It is a view that is often, and rightly, criticised as simplistic. There is a more dialectical relation between social relations and technology, the critics say, and, as such, it is hard to state which determines which.

In the popular literature on Australian multiculturalism one can find a similarly formulaic view that can be termed 'policy determinism'. While those on the right of the political spectrum make statements such as 'the policy of assimilation gave us the cohesive and well-integrated society and the policy of multiculturalism gave us the fragmented society of ethnic communities', those on the left reply 'the policy of assimilation gave us racism while the policy of multiculturalism gave us the ethnically plural and cosmopolitan society'. While many are willing to argue with the particular details of these statements, it is surprising how few venture into a critique of their overall logic and the way they fetishise cultural policy and give it such unrealistic powers of shaping society. Apparently, regardless of what is happening on the ground, society is magically transformed almost immediately after a change in government policy.

That things do not happen this way is not very hard to prove if any proof were needed. For instance, even a cursory historical investigation of the 1970s, with an eye on actual social developments on the ground and not just policy, can show that far from 'creating' ethnic communities, multiculturalism evolved as a reaction to their growth. However, the very obvious fact that ethnic communities began emerging under the policy of assimilation is not something that those who, in the face of supposed multicultural fragmentation, are today arguing for a 'return to assimilation' like to contemplate. Certainly, multiculturalism later facilitated the growth and institutionalisation of such communities, but it remains important to say that multiculturalism came about because ethnic communities emerged rather than the opposite.

Policy being an instrument of government, the pressure to change it begins when governments feel it is not performing its governing role. This is when it faces, or even becomes complicit in producing, 'the ungovernable': that which cannot be conceived, let alone governed, from within given institutions responsible for defining social issues or problems and designing and implementing policy to deal with them. From this perspective we can restate the claim of the preceding paragraph in this way: far from being the product of multiculturalism, ethnic communities were in fact the ungovernable of the cultural policy of immigrant assimilation. Assimilation operated with the assumption that immigrants were assimilable and as such worked towards achieving this goal with the expectations that this is what immigrants do. It appeared to work while migrants were newly arrived, isolated, small in number and happy to conform and keep the non-assimilable part of themselves locked in cupboards. But as migration increased, and migrants found themselves amongst their own, the desire and the capacity to publicly retain aspects of one's culture became easier to express and 'ethnic communities' started taking shape. They slowly became the ungovernable of assimilation policy in that the tools made available to the government as it was oriented by assimilation could not even define the 'problem' of ethnic communities conceptually, let alone deploy its apparatus to govern it.

Ungovernability is not an essential quality of the object to be governed. It is a quality that emerges when something escapes the relation between a government apparatus and what it is aiming to govern. When a process or a social group is deemed ungovernable it is both a reflection of certain qualities and features that the process or the group possesses and that makes it hard to govern and a reflection of the capacity and the limitations of the government apparatus to deploy itself on it, capture it conceptually and institutionally, and govern it.

I want to concentrate on the case of Australia's cultural policy towards immigrants to argue that Muslim immigrants in the West have become the ungovernable of the multicultural governmental apparatus. I will show that in being constructed as such they reflect, as mentioned above, certain qualities and features that 'Muslims in the West' possess and that makes them ungovernable, as well as something about the governmental power of the Western nation-state today.

Muslims in Australia

Historically speaking, Muslims have not been considered Australia's most threatening other. Even as late as the 1990s, and while the Muslim other became increasingly important following the first Gulf War, Australia's core threatening other remained (what it has always been) Asians, which in Australia meant primarily South-East Asian. While in terms of international threats Muslim Indonesia has always loomed large, it was more the fact that Indonesia was an underdeveloped and populous rather than an Islamic nation that mattered most. When the racist movement of Pauline Hanson emerged in the mid-1990s, there was hardly a mention of Muslims, and the Asians were still its primary target.

It was only at the turn of the century that the Muslims became the primary threat. It can be said that this period saw a globalisation of the Islamic other around the world. And like all processes of cultural globalisation, it involves contradictory processes of homogenisation and heterogenisation of a cultural trend.[1] Thus while Islam was becoming homogenised as the global threatening other, the category that embodied the Islamic threat differed from one country to another: Asians in Britain (there meaning Indians and Pakistanis), Turks in Germany and North Africans in France. In Australia it is the category Lebanese that came to embody this threat. Although in the early nineteenth century and until the middle of the twentieth century Lebanese migration to Australia was primarily Christian, the number of Muslim Lebanese began to rise considerably from the 1960s onward. More importantly, the Lebanese migrants of the 1960s, 1970s and 1980s were unskilled and with very low level of education. They were initially recruited into an industrial sector (particularly the automobile industry) that was soon to be decimated, and they soon suffered massive unemployment. Because of their lack of educational and cultural resources (relative to the Australian context) this unemployment became chronic: it was inherited across generations. Muslim Lebanese today have the highest rate of unemployment in the country. This also meant that an underclass culture structured around various black economies flourished among them and featured highly mediatised gang formations dubbed Middle Eastern or Lebanese gangs.

This Lebanese Muslim tale of the rise of an economically disadvantaged community with a small criminal element attached to it was not in itself unique in Australian history. Nor was it something that Australian multiculturalism found particularly difficult to encompass. Indeed there are many communities that have shown similar patterns of disadvantage and criminality and have nevertheless become an integral part of the Australian 'multicultural family'. To understand their emergence as ungovernable we need to look elsewhere.

The Faith of the Other

The first element that contributed to a conception of 'the Muslim' as outside the multicultural realm is the existence of a substantial and increasing number of 'seriously religious' people. To be seriously religious here does not simply mean going frequently to the mosque or holding intense religious beliefs. It does not even denote a high degree of enthusiasm. More importantly, it means considering *all aspects* of one's everyday life as ruled by the laws of one's God.[2] It is this kind of religiosity, particularly when it is the religiosity of the other, that constitutes a serious negation of the logic of multiculturalism. Multiculturalism has always found a way, indeed it can be defined by an ability, to find room for minor elements of the law of the other to exist within the dominant national law—here I don't necessarily mean law in a formal sense, though it could be, but more an anthropological conception of law as 'the other's order of things' or 'the other's way of life'. In this sense, we can say that multiculturalism is primarily defined by this relation of encompassment. The dominant national law opens a space, a state of exception if you will, where the law of the other can exist for as long as it is encompassed by the national law. The space where the law of the other exists can vary in content and in magnitude, but what cannot possibly change is that the dominant culture has to be the encompassing culture and the law of the other the encompassed culture.

The problem that arises with seriously religious Muslims is that what they see as their laws are nothing short of the Laws of God. These are not equivalent to minor laws such the rules of a specific national cuisine or even the ethno-specific laws of marriage and kinship. The idea that you can have a space where you can speak your language, eat your food and follow your rituals for as long as you understand that this is a space offered to you, so to speak, by the dominant language, the dominant mode of eating, etc. is relatively unproblematic. But the idea of having the laws of the nation offer a space for the Laws of God is sacrilegious. Indeed, for people who take their religion seriously, the situation is reversed. It is the Laws of God that are the all-encompassing ones and the national laws of the host nation, or any other nation for that matter, that are the minor ones. For a seriously religious Muslim migrant integration in the host nation becomes a matter of finding a space for these national laws within the all-encompassing Laws of God. The very relation between a dominant encompassing culture and a minor encompassed culture on which multiculturalism is based is here inverted and intimations of ungovernability start to arise. But this is not where they end. That some Muslims think of themselves as belonging to a politicised transnational community or *Umma* has given a further earthly flavour to this mode of living under the Laws of God, transforming it into a kind of metaphysical transnationalism.

What has made the difference are the international political developments that articulated themselves to both Islamic transnationalism and to the local patterns of Islamic disadvantage such as those described earlier. The starting point of these developments and what perhaps remains the main important one is the rise of Iran as an Islamic nation. This has since led to the development of various forms of global Islamic politics including Islamic terrorism.

The Iranian revolution instituted for the first time a rule of law that openly portrays itself as a kind of transcendent Muslim political will. Subsequently, this political will was perceived for the first time to exercise itself transnationally with the Salman Rushdie affair. As if suddenly Muslims were in a position to openly sentence a person living in and subject to the protection of the law of a Western nation-state. Even more threatening to the Western national will, numerous Muslims who were supposed to be its subjects show themselves to be the agents of the transnational Muslim will by calling for the carrying out of, or volunteering to carry out, the sentence themselves. Since that time, there have been many occasions where Muslims have shown themselves to be the subjects of a transnational will that is other to the West, with September 11 and the London bombings leading to the perception of the Islamic will not just as the will of the other, but as the will of the enemy. It is this, more than anything else, that has put Muslims outside the realm of what multicultural politics can deal with. For multiculturalism was always about finding a space for the culture of the other in so far as this culture does not claim a sovereignty over itself that clashes with the laws of the nation.

On Misinterpellation

Another important social trend that puts some Muslims outside multicultural governmentality is Islam becoming a space of protection from racism when racism is not dealt with efficiently by multiculturalism.

Some of the most-circulated comments following the London terrorist bombing had to do with the fact that the London bombers were second-generation immigrants: 'homegrown', as everyone was claiming in disbelief. This was taken to demonstrate how unassimilated London's South Asians are given that not even the second generation is assimilated. What the relationship is between not being assimilated and hatred is not very clear. Lack of assimilation produces lack of interest and lack of emotion towards the culture one has not assimilated to. To express such strong and destructive feelings towards a place comes from intense and even intimate interaction with it. That is, hatred does not come from lack of assimilation. If anything it comes from a frustrated and unrecognised sense of over-assimilation. It comes from an experience of rejection. This is not to say that there is a necessary link between terrorism and the second generation. It is to say that if one has to pick a candidate for being a terrorist full of hatred towards the host country, it is far more likely that the person will be a second rather than a first generation.

It is worth noting here that everywhere the dominant

multicultural or liberal Western culture is having problems with Muslims, whether France, Denmark, England or Australia, the problem is primarily linked to youth. This is because, as many works with immigrants have shown, the second generation is likely to experience not only a different but also a more intense sense of injury from racism than did the first generation.[3] Here lies one of the problems with multiculturalism as an anti-racist ideology limited to a form of ideological anti-Eurocentrism. As I have argued in detail in *White Nation*,[4] multiculturalism is generally very limited as an anti-racist policy. It never stops reproducing the centrality of white Europeans' entitlement to the nation. Nevertheless, multicultural recognition as a form of anti-Eurocentrism and valorisation of the other's culture can be seen as a form of anti-racism. The issue I want to deal with here is that this form of multicultural anti-racism is far more geared to dealing with migrants who are relatively new to their host country. The pain of not being recognised or being recognised negatively is a predominantly first-generation experience. Furthermore, there is a sense in which the first generation expect the racism directed towards them. Indeed, in my own fieldwork, I often hear migrants engaging in discourses aiming to legitimate the racism towards them. They say things like: 'I would have done the same, if they had come to my country' and 'well, it is their country...you know, we have to accept that'. The second generation, on the other hand, become, if anything, oversensitive to any kind of exclusionary behaviour directed towards them. Because they always get a whiff of the racism experienced by their parents before them, but more importantly, because, unlike their parents, they experience racism from an early age, and because this racism is directed at them with a language and culture that is their own, they develop an excessive and even a reactive idealised sense of entitlement to non-discriminatory treatment. This is what I meant by over-assimilated: they develop an idealised sense of non-discriminatory belonging that even nonracialised citizens have no access to. Through a long history of being on the receiving end of everyday modes of being demeaned, ostracised and excluded they develop a kind of habitus, a well-attuned capacity to recognise or to sniff all those small insignificant modes of mostly petty, subtle and unsubtle, direct and indirect, implicit and explicit, and voluntary and involuntary exclusionary behaviours that become part of their everyday lives. It is this everyday petty racism coupled with the exaggerated sense of entitlement that can swell up into a sometimes formidable state of resentment that is very different in intensity from the sentiment felt by first-generation immigrants when faced with racism.

A slightly transformed notion of ideological interpellation that Althusser developed long ago can help us theorise and get a better analytical grasp of the difference between the experiences of first generation and second generation immigrants. For Althusser, the notion of interpellation helps explain the social formation of subjects within society. Althusser was inspired by a Lacanian tale that went roughly as follows: the way parents talk about their forthcoming baby, prepare his or her room, and start planning their lives as if the baby is already present, creates a symbolic space that actually awaits the baby to simply come and occupy it. In Althusser's conception of subject formation, society operates in the same way. It has already allocated symbolic structural locations, such as 'worker', which simply hail or interpellate a person to fill the already existing space. The moment a person is hailed and comes to occupy a certain position is the moment that gives meaning to their lives.[5]

From this perspective racism is a failure in the interpellation system, whereby society falls short of allocating the racialised person a space that makes their life meaningful. But this failure varies. It can be said that the first-generation immigrants experience a racism that takes either the form of non-interpellation or the form of a negative interpellation. To be nationally non-interpellated is to find no space for yourself in the ideological plane which constitutes people as subjects of a particular nation. This is the drama of non-recognition: you do not feel you are being hailed from anywhere. Non-recognition produces invisibility and a yearning to be noticed and acknowledged. Negative interpellation is different. It does not lead to invisibility. Rather it is the visibility produced by classical modes of racist inferiorisation. This is where migrants say of their racist experience 'I was treated like an animal', meaning a form of recognition, but recognition of someone as less than human. While the second generation can experience the above forms of racism, its primary experience is one of misinterpellation. This is far more dramatic and emotionally complex than being negatively interpellated. For here, the person recognises themselves as being interpellated only to find out that they are not. When the nation hails you 'hey you citizen', everything in you leads you to recognise that it is you that is being hailed, but when you do say 'yes it is me', you experience the shock of the rejection where the very ideological grid that is inviting you in the nation expels you through the petty and not so petty acts of exclusion that racists engage in in their everyday lives. You say 'it is me' and the ideological structure of society replies with cruelty: 'No. Piss off. It is not you I am calling.' Subjection to racism always involves an experience of fragmentation. When this subjection is intense as in the case of misinterpellation it can become an experience of shattering. And while a fragmented subject can always manage to pull themselves together to be operational in the world, the shattered racialised person needs a space immune from the effect of racism in order to pick up the pieces as it were. It is here that Islamic religion has been playing an important role among Muslim youth in the West that multiculturalism has not and cannot play.

Being directed at promoting both the recognition of the culture of the other and the valorisation of this culture, it can be said that multiculturalism has always been geared to deal with the forms of exclusion and lack of recognition that emanate from non-interpellation and negative interpellation. It has not been conceived to handle the drama of misinterpellation. As such it often leaves the second generation outside its operative sphere, as it were, and as such positions them, yet again, as ungovernable. This is not surprising. For the misinterpellated is not someone yearning to have their culture recognised. It is someone who was yearning to assimilate, someone who has offered the nation his or her assimilation, but the nation through a variety of racist subjects has rejected it. Many such subjects suffer from what I have called 'assimilation fatigue'. They become sick of trying to assimilate as a mode of defining themselves in viable terms. Instead, they start looking outside official ideologies to each other (gangs), to music (rap) or, as is the case among many Muslim youth, to religion to find a space where they can develop a viable sense of themselves and to immunise themselves against the constant threat of psychological disintegration that racism constitutes for them.

For those youths of Muslim background who turn to religion in this way, Islam becomes the anti-racist ideology, *par excellence*. It offers a space where they can develop a healthy conception of themselves as opposed to the negatively racialised one that is constantly thrown at them by the rest of society. This works to reinforce the process of non-encompassment described above. Islam starts standing opposite multiculturalism as a competing governmentality rather than as a culture that can be governed by it.

For reasons of narrative clarity and to highlight the question of misinterpellation, I have argued perhaps simplistically that the racialised second generation become more sensitive to the racism directed towards them. While this is true, it is also true, and paradoxically so, that they can also routinise certain forms of negative treatment and see them as part of the way they come to belong. If first-generation immigrants come to accept racism because they feel that they do not belong, the second generation can come to accept certain forms of marginalisation as the very way they belong to Australia. Misinterpellation is the experience only of those who fantasised that they can totally belong within the dominant culture. There are many others who slowly carve out a belonging within the nation but outside the dominant culture. That is, they find a space within the nation where they nationally interpellate themselves as misinterpellated. This has also been a marked tendency among second-generation Muslim youth who are not particularly religious. The way this routinisation of marginality puts the whole apparatus of multiculturalism in question was highlighted in the dramatic Cronulla events in Sydney.

Cronulla and the Crisis of the Multicultural-Assimilationist Apparatus

In December 2005, a crowd of around 5000 white, mainly male, Australians was mobilised to descend on one of Sydney's most popular beaches, Cronulla beach, and 'reclaim it' from Muslims, Lebanese and wogs. The crowd chased and violently attacked a number of lone individuals deemed to be of Middle Eastern descent (this apparently included a Greek and a Bangladeshi).

The immediate trigger of the events was an altercation a week before between a couple of Lebanese Muslim youths and two lifesavers in which the latter ended up being severely bashed. This event itself followed a history of tensions between the largely white locals and non-local Muslim Lebanese men who were increasingly perceived to have 'taken over', imposing their forms of masculinity (modes of playing football and modes of harassing girls) on the beach. But given the lifesaver's iconic status in Australian society, the bashing was constructed as the crossing of a line beyond what can be tolerated and as another example of the Muslims' arrogant disregard of and disrespect towards Australian values. This is a theme that has been continually expressed by various public commentators over the last few years. Thus, what followed the bashing was public outrage expressed in, and fomented by, parts of the populist media (tabloids and talk-back radio). This same media gave high exposure to the various calls to reclaim the beach that circulated through SMS messaging. Well-known racist, right-wing fringe groups also mobilised and exploited the situation.

Far from being only the result of a tension between white Australians and Australians of Lebanese background, the Cronulla events are also a reflection of a crisis in Australia's capacity to govern and incorporate Muslim immigrants in Australia. The very nature of the rioting crowd pointed towards the crisis. Unlike other global events such as the LA or the Paris riots, this was not rioting by yet another racialised, socially disadvantaged and marginalised group. Here, the rioters were whites from the dominant Anglo-Celtic culture chasing people belonging to a minority. As some analysts have put it, this was in the tradition of pogroms not the tradition of riots.[6] And pogroms are indicators of a specific kind of governmental tension. They are performed by individuals from a cultural grouping within society that see themselves as dominant enough to feel capable of legitimately taking the law in their own hands as an expression of what they see as the failure of the state to act in their name. In Cronulla, the white crowd had a strong sense of entitlement that the beach was theirs, that they knew what the right way to behave on the beach was, and that they were entitled to judge who was behaving properly and who was not. At one level, the white crowd deployed itself to perform what it felt the government should have performed but failed to do: preserve a specific Australian way of life. What is interesting is that not all the crowd saw this specific way of life that needs to be protected as a monocultural one: some spoken to by various reporters saw themselves defending a multicultural way of life that they believed the Muslims were ruining. It was as if the exterminatory impulse that moved the crowd, and that was there for all to see in the way it surrounded and pounced on its Lebanese/Muslim prey, was itself the result of an impasse generated neither by the crisis of multiculturalism eagerly declared by some, nor by the crisis of monocultural assimilationism, but the crisis of the very governmentality that was based on a supposed choice between the two.

Here we come to an important point. In many parts of the world, but particularly in Australia, multiculturalism is portrayed as an alternative to and a transcendence of monocultural assimilation. This to a certain extent is obviously true. But it also obscures a very important fact. Multicultural governance has always relied on the continued existence of an assimilationist tendency at the very heart of multiculturalism in order to achieve its aims. All government documents on multiculturalism from the foundational Galbally report[7] onwards celebrate diversity but ensure with a 'but' or an 'as long as' or 'in so far as' that no one forgets that this diversity should not happen at the cost of Australia's cohesion, core values, etc. Assimilationism, therefore, always existed as a disciplinary technique which was deployed specifically to ensure that the diverse cultures that were integrated into the multicultural fold were 'good to integrate and be multicultural about' in the first place. If multiculturalism was deployed to teach immigrant horses how to be mounted by those who wanted to enjoy their culture, assimilation was the technique deployed to break them before such training. It is in this sense that we can realistically speak of a multicultural-assimilationist apparatus. It is an apparatus in which multiculturalism and assimilation were positioned respectively in the guise of carrots and sticks: even at the very height of multiculturalism, assimilation was continuously deployed, either through a government report, or a politician's statement or even sometimes through popular mobilisation, as a way of domesticating 'the wild side' of certain communities and as the very pre-condition of them entering the multicultural realm: 'You are welcome but leave your conflicts behind', 'We are enriched by this aspect of your culture but not that', etc. Those who are polemically inclined should note here that I am not saying that it was necessarily a bad governmental policy because of this. Perhaps even this combination of multiculturalism and assimilation was the most appropriate policy that the government could take at the time. Nonetheless, it remains worthwhile to note that the very condition of multicultural governmentality worked through fostering an ideological polarity between assimilation and multiculturalism while, practically speaking, both policies were intimately related in the same governmental apparatus.

This is why those who see the Cronulla events as a crisis of multiculturalism and offer the need for more assimilation fail to see how dramatic a crisis Cronulla represents. After all, it is important to remember that Cronulla emerged not at the height of multicultural fervour but following ten years of fostering anti-multicultural assimilationist rhetoric by the highly conservative government of John Howard, the bulk of which was directed at Muslims whether as immigrants with a settlement problem, or as 'illegal refugees' who are barbaric enough to throw their children overboard or uncivilised enough to jump the queue.

Marwan, a young man of Lebanese background I interviewed after the Cronulla event, had a story about what happened to one of the Lebanese men who got bashed on the beach: 'After punching him to the ground, this bloke got on top of him and shoved the Australian flag in his face and said "kiss the flag". The [Lebanese] guy said "but that's my flag". The bloke on top him said "No its not. Kiss the flag."'

Given the number of mythical stories that have circulated about Cronulla, I have no way of verifying that this happened. Nor has Marwan, though he firmly believes that it did. But like all mythical stories it denotes a structure of experience well beyond the immediate event. And this story reveals how the young Lebanese-Australian men on the beach experience the dead-end of the forced assimilationism exhibited by some of the crowd who fantasised themselves doing the job of taming the Muslims that multiculturalism was supposedly not doing. The assimilationists tell their other: 'Assimilate'. But if the other says: 'But I am assimilated', the assimilationist simply ignores this and says: 'No you're not. Assimilate!' It is well known that the monocultural assimilationists are never interested in the assimilation of the other. Rather, they are interested in portraying them to be in need of assimilation. This shows itself in assimilationist politics again and again. But at Cronulla the assimilationist demand reached another degree of absurdity and it takes us close to how the Cronulla 'Leb boys' saw themselves and how they were seen by both the multiculturalists and the monoculturalists.

The cultural forms exhibited by some of the Lebanese-Australian youths on the beach that became generalised as 'Lebanese behaviour' and irked so many people were clearly a hybrid formation: the forms of working or under-class masculinity that were put on show were a touch Lebanese, but nothing that you can find exhibited in this way in Lebanon, except perhaps among Lebanese Australians living in Lebanon! They also contained a touch of the black and Latino American cultural subaltern hype that has been globalised by the mass media through the propagation of particular types of music, clothing, walking, etc. And they were in other ways quintessentially Australian—working class Australian perhaps, but Australian nonetheless.

However, what is striking about the youths is not so much the fact that they lived in a marginal working or under-class hybrid culture but how *at ease* they were with their working or under-class hybridity: they shamelessly exhibited it. They were totally comfortable on the beach being sexist, being macho, being vulgar and being aggressive. They were really very much at home. It is in this that they placed themselves outside the multicultural-monocultural field of governmentality. They rubbed the multiculturalists the wrong way because they did not represent a valuable culture that one can be multicultural about: no Anglo-cosmopolitan multiculturalist looked at them and thought: 'I am enriched by your presence in my country.' But then, the Lebanese-Australian youths couldn't care less; they were looking neither for recognition nor for valorisation. And they were certainly not looking for tolerance. They just assumed that they could merely be Australian in the way they had grown to be. Paradoxically, this is where they rubbed the monocultural assimilationists the wrong way. For on one hand they seemed like obvious candidates for the 'assimilationist stick', a stick that can tame them and make them ready to enter multiculturalism and start cooking some Lebanese food rather than desiring and harassing Aussie women in a vulgar way. But those youths had no sense of needing to assimilate to anything. It is at this point that the absurdity, and also the hypocrisy, of deploying assimilation on them emerges. For beneath the complaint that the youths were not well-assimilated and well-integrated was really the fear that the youths acted as if they were completely assimilated and integrated *despite* their cultural marginality and difference. They were assimilated on their own terms. They were not Australians in the way others wanted them to be, but they nonetheless felt themselves fully and *unproblematically* Australian. And this is exactly what triggers the monocultural assimilationist fear inherent in the 'No this is not your flag. Kiss the flag' myth and its successive, apparently contradictory injunctions: 'How dare you say you are Australian. No you're not Australian. Become Australian.' What is behind the claims that the Lebanese youths were unintegrated was the fear that they seemed *overintegrated*. For people who are so different they were too integrated for their own good: they had no sense of their assumed marginality: arrogant. 'We don't expect you to act like this on the beach,' the assimilationists and the multiculturalists were screaming in unison. 'Can't you be a bit shy for God's sake! You should feel like hiding your feelings when you are desiring an Aussie chick on the beach in *this* way.' Here was a lament that is an established and on-going feature of all forms of racialised relations of power, already well-known to slave owners when addressing their slaves who looked a touch too long at 'the lady': how dare you exhibit your desire from your position of difference and marginality! It is in this that the Lebanese-Australian youths exhibited their ungovernability in the face of the multicultural-assimilationist duo that were often deployed *in tandem* to ensure the integration of people in Australian culture.

The problem with these youths was that—born in Australia, in an Australian-grown (albeit hybrid and racialised) culture—they seem to have lost the sense of their marginality in that culture. Or, more correctly, they feel totally Australian in their very marginality. That is, *they felt marginalised within Australia not from Australia*, and many are often surprised to hear their Australian-ness being questioned. This is something that often comes up in my ethnographic and interview material. And it was the case in the interviews I conducted after Cronulla.

'How did you feel when the riots happened?' I asked Marwan. 'In all honesty, many of my mates were shocked... we grew up having all kind of confrontations with many of these blokes...there's one of them I still see on the beach. I punched him when he was ten or eleven,' he said.

Marwan speaks as if the little periodical confrontations they had with the 'these blokes' on the beach over many years were part of his Australian culture. So, to have a confrontation that brings all confrontations to an end was kind of unAustralian. 'I was shocked,' he kept repeating. To get stuck into each other ritually was fine: 'we knew it will happen again on the next weekend,' he said. It was as if somehow being hated by 'the Aussies' was how Marwan saw himself and his friends being interpellated as Australians on the beach. Strangely, it was a position he felt comfortable with. What he couldn't cope with was that the riots were not part of the game: they were aiming to end the game and end his position within it. That took him and his friends by surprise and hurt him in ways that losing a fight on one of the routine days on the beach did not. The riots were not aiming at portraying him negatively. They were aiming at terminating his very physical presence and symbolic existence on the beach.

Beyond the Multiculturalism-Assimilation Polarity

In the first part of this essay, I began by pointing out that what makes a governmental object 'ungovernable' is not only the qualities it possesses but the capacities of the governing group as well: ungovernability is the relation between the two. While the nature of the Muslims' current radical encounter with multiculturalism should not be underestimated, this in itself does not explain how they have become ungovernable. Nor does it explain the intensity of the reaction and the fears that their ungovernability arouses. What explains this intensity is the fact that the white Australian culture that is facing this Islamic other is marred by a sense of insecurity that has emerged independently of the Islamic question. This sense of insecurity is rooted in the way the process of globalisation has rendered fragile people's structural integration into their nation-states.

When multiculturalism emerged, it aimed to integrate people from cultural minorities into the nation-state. The integration of people from the dominant culture was never considered an issue. It was taken for granted. This was a time when a nation meant primarily a national economy. By having a job people were already integrated in the nation. And when they didn't, the welfare state gave them that a sense of integration. Globalisation and neo-liberal policies have meant that in many instances the economy has detached itself from the nation. To be located within the economy does not necessarily locate you within the nation. This has meant that one's position within the nation is increasingly predicated on the domain of identity and culture. It has also meant that for many whites the sense of belonging to the nation has become brittle. Their need to reaffirm the nation's identity in terms of the culture of the majority rather than in relativist terms has become increasingly important. White European culture has been increasingly experienced as besieged, maligned, relativised and devalued in the face of third-world cultures that were, in the eyes of white nationalists, inferior. It is in this context that a sentiment of 'we've had enough of silently copping the behaviour of this third-world Muslim minority imposing its uncivilised standards of behaviour on us when we know that our standards of behaviour are so much better' becomes prevalent.

In that sense, the actions of the white Australians of Cronulla beach echoes many other forms of white reactions to Muslims across the globe, including the infamous 'Muhammad cartoons' debacle.[8] These incidents and many others are manifestations of a growing need among sections of the white populations of the West to reassert and reaffirm both their majority status and the superiority of their European values in the face of what they see as an Islamic, but also more generally a multicultural relativist, threat.

The problem is that this reassertion, because it is in a sense imprisoned by the 'multiculturalism-assimilation polarity', can only lead to the kind of dead-ends that the Cronulla events have led to. It has become crucial to find ways of moving beyond such a polarity. Yet this will not be easy, even when moving in the usual domain of identity politics, for while continuing to assert the plurality of our societies, it is important not to fall into a relativism which forbids us from asserting an attachment to certain social gains made in Western societies as truly universal gains. And while affirming the importance of an openness on otherness and a willingness to accommodate its demands, it is crucial that this effort is reciprocated: there is nothing wrong with the other, so to speak, they can make an effort to accommodate the demands of the dominant culture and change too. But it seems to me clear that the most important leap that government policy will need to make is that the demands of otherness are no longer about the recognition of identity-based cultural differences but a capacity to incorporate the plurality of ways in which humans pursue what they consider a viable life. Such demands are difficult because they invite not just a new policy in the usual sense but a reconsideration of the very way the Western nation-state has conceived of its sovereignty.

MULTICULTURALISM, LOVE OF COUNTRY AND RESPONSES TO TERRORISM

Raimond Gaita

RAIMOND GAITA

is Emeritus Professor of Moral Philosophy at King's College London, and Professorial Fellow at Melbourne Law School and the Faculty of Arts, University of Melbourne. His books include *Good and Evil: An Absolute Conception, Romulus, My Father, A Common Humanity, The Philosopher's Dog, Why the War Was Wrong* (ed.), *Breach of Trust: Truth, Morality and Politics (Quarterly Essay 16)* and *Gaza: Morality, Law and Politics* (ed.).

Multiculturalism comes in many varieties. The same is true of the difficulties multicultural nations now face in parts of Europe and elsewhere. Multiculturalism has been attacked from many political positions, though perhaps most noticeably from the right. From that perspective, multiculturalism, with its allegedly relativistic assumptions about value, looks to have eviscerated national pride and created a moral and spiritual emptiness that Islamic militants have exploited. But criticism has also come from the left and from classical Millsian liberals. Writing in the London *Independent* on behalf of a Britain he hoped would again be inspired by the liberal philosophy of John Stuart Mill, Johann Hari praised, with savage irony, the recommendation by the Archbishop of Canterbury, Rowan Williams, that British Muslims live under aspects of Sharia law. Evidently Hari hoped that not even multiculturalism could survive such foolishness.

I hope that I won't disappoint readers if I stay at some

distance from those arguments. I want to avoid many of the false alternatives that cultural warriors from the left and the right, but mainly from the right, have pressed on us. If it is an exaggeration, then it is one with a point to say that the call after September 11 to reassess the value of multiculturalism, which became in fact a call to assess the assimilability of Muslims, was also, at least in Australia where Muslims pose no serious threat, an opportunity for cultural warriors from the right to reignite a longstanding argument with the left over multiculturalism—an argument that had really nothing to do with the so called 'war on terror'.

Be that as it may: I am not an historian, nor a social scientist of any kind. I'm a philosopher, so I want to reflect on some of the ideas that inform the belief that successful multiculturalism *must* undermine an attachment to nation that goes deeper than dutiful citizenship, an attachment that at its best and deepest deserves to be called love of country.

It helps, I think, to get that anxiety in perspective, to see that unsettling questions about national identity would have arisen for Australians if not one immigrant had set foot in this country. Slow though it was to take effect here, the impact of the worldwide movement against racism that began with the response to the Holocaust and was deepened by retreat—literal and moral—from colonialism, forced Australians to acknowledge the injustices that were and continue to be committed against the indigenous inhabitants of this continent. Understanding what it means to be Australian could not have remained unchanged. Australians had no choice but to think hard about the nature of collective responsibility, about the relations between guilt, pride and shame, about the standards that should inform judgment of other cultures and about whether it is always dangerous for national loyalty to seek a basis deeper than common citizenship. We had no choice, that is, if we were to be truthful about our history and, therefore, who we are.

Now that the Aborigines have received their apology, it remains to be seen how they will think politically about their culture. It seems evident that insofar as the rootedness—such as it remains—of Aboriginal peoples in their distinctive cultures should be honoured and encouraged to flourish, they cannot be treated as a multicultural group among others. To do so would be to treat them as though they are not seriously to be distinguished from immigrants. To the extent that Aboriginal leaders resisted calls to assimilation, they invited non-indigenous Australians to discuss forms of political association that would be true to the history of their dispossession, forms that would be to some degree, and probably unnervingly, novel to the history of Western political thought. Acceptance of that invitation would take more generosity and a deeper sense of justice than the nation appears even now to possess.

While it would be absurd to regard the place of Aboriginal cultures in Australia as being in principle no different from the place of Italian or Greek culture, it is also absurd, as John Hirst pointed out (in *Sense and Nonsense in Australian History*), to say that we are *all* immigrants, implying thereby that only the Aborigines justifiably enjoy the status previously accorded to Anglo-Celts when they were contrasted with the immigrants.[1] An immigrant is not just a new arrival to an inhabited land: she is a new arrival to an established political order. In the continent of Australia, Anglo-Celts created the relevant political order and (eventually) called it Australia. With the exception of refugees, immigrants came there not by right, but in response to an invitation by a nation that could justifiably refuse them entry. What that justification comes to, how we should conceptualise it and how far it extends—these are, rightly, more controversial issues now than they were in the 1940s and 50s, but hardly anyone seriously proposes that nation-states should be denied legitimate power to refuse immigrants entry. The Anglo-Celts were not immigrants, partly because they were de facto conquerors, but also because there was no Australia conceived as a political entity, or anything like it, for them to be immigrants into. To call the indigenous people of the continent 'the first

Australians' is, as I think John Hirst also pointed out, to create confusion.

Both as ideology and a naturally emerging fact in the life of the nation, multiculturalism in Australia developed as a movement against assimilation as many Australians conceived it in the 1950s, but in neither form was it a call to negotiate for immigrants' distinctive forms of political association within Australia, in the way that calls for a treaty and for self-determination were for the Aborigines. Were it to have been such a call, most Australians would have been justifiably resentful.

Attention to a topical example will help me to explain why I believe their resentment would have been justified. There is a strong case for respecting Aboriginal customary law and for sometimes allowing it to take precedence over Commonwealth or State laws when the behaviour it judges and punishes does not breach universal human rights as they are set out in international law, or does not in other ways undermine the law of the land. When talk of self-determination implied, as I suggested earlier, the exploration of possibly novel forms of political association that would truthfully express the Aborigines' dispossession, then acceptance of aspects of customary law was taken to be fundamental to the definition of whatever distinctive political identity Aborigines would forge together with non-indigenous Australians. That it should be so was taken to be part of the morally and politically complex acknowledgment by non-indigenous Australians of the fact that their political ancestors had dispossessed indigenous Australians of their lands. No comparable case can be made for allowing Sharia law, for example, to define for Australian Muslims a distinctive political identity. Because immigrants come as guests who may eventually become citizens, the host country has the right, as well as a duty to its citizens, to require that immigrants do not claim for their religion a political status in the life of the nation different from the status of any other religion except the national religion, if there is one.

That does not imply that religion should be relegated to the private realm, as Rowan Williams appeared to believe when he warned of 'the marginalisation of certain kinds of affiliations, or their privatisation, in which particular sorts of reasoning are tolerated as private matters only, but never granted legitimacy in public as part of a continuing debate about shared goods and priorities'.[2] Between the political and the private realms there is much space for many different kinds of public institutions.

I remarked earlier that when Australians and foreigners praise Australia for being a successful multicultural nation, they do not think it has successfully implemented an ideology or theory of multiculturalism, nor even, I suspect, that it has successfully implemented policy of the kind that finds expression in the creation of, for example, SBS. They mean, I think, that immigrants can hope to prosper here, that there is little hostility to them and that they are (on the whole) accorded the respect that expresses the recognition that they can love and be loyal to Australia while also loving their country of origin in whose culture they are still rooted and which still nourishes them.

Virtually everyone acknowledges that if loyalties clash, as they sometimes do, then, at the crunch, in some matters of foreign policy and certainly in time of war, other loyalties must not seriously conflict with loyalty to Australia. Refusal of that loyalty would be punished in ways appropriate to the refusal. In the extreme case, a naturalised immigrant who took up arms against his nation would be charged with an offence whose proper name is treason. If he weren't naturalised then he would be deported if the circumstances of doing so were consistent with his rights under international law. Appeal to the values of multiculturalism could hardly be entered as defence of treason, let alone provide a reason for refusing its application to an immigrant Australian or for jettisoning the concept altogether. But, of course, what will count as treason, indeed, what will count as a serious conflict of loyalties, will itself be a function of what one thinks it means to belong to a multicultural nation. There is, I think, no morally and politically neutral theory of the nation or of citizenship waiting to be developed that will enable us to adjudicate the problems of multiculturalism. And there is no neutral theory of multiculturalism that will enable us to adjudicate the problems of nationalism and loyal citizenship.

In the 1950s the experience of most immigrants was less benign. They often suffered condescension, were expected to assimilate quickly, or, if they couldn't, then to behave in ways that showed that they knew they should try; by, for example, not speaking their mother tongue in public. Languages other than English were sometimes ridiculed as though they hadn't really achieved the dignity of language, as though they were merely pretenders to it. Given the deep connections between language, thought and feeling, it is no small matter effectively to denigrate someone's native tongue, the language in which someone had discovered herself, and to discourage families, lovers and friends from speaking it to one another in public.

The condescension shown towards 'New Australians', as they were called, often rankled with them. Sometimes it hurt and humiliated. Seldom, however, did immigrants suffer much worse. Those I knew as a boy and later were grateful for the relative tolerance shown to them by people whom they unhesitatingly called, not old Australians, but simply Australians. (Considered as a polemical point intended to deflate the Anglo-Celts, the claim that we are all immigrants would have struck them as absurd.) Most of them knew only too painfully the difference between condescension and thoughtless humiliation, and the bitter hatreds that had torn apart the countries from which they came. As well as identifying themselves as Yugoslavs, or Italians or Poles and so on, they would identify themselves as Europeans to distinguish themselves from Australians. But whether they were victims, accomplices or merely bystanders to the Nazi genocide or Soviet mass murder, they knew Europe was the continent where nations were so disfigured by murderous hatreds that often—as in the case of the German resistance—true patriots rightly believed their obligation to fight against their governments to be the deepest expression of their patriotism. For that reason, most of the immigrants I knew accepted as a gift, rather than claimed as a right, the liberty and tolerance they found here. John Hirst is right to say that the immigrants did not bring this tolerance to Australia. European immigrants who fled tyranny have a strong commitment to freedom that is often matched by a failure to understand—in their bones, so to speak—the delicate and fragile nature of democratic institutions and practices insofar as they are governed by such conventions. It can take little to provoke them to calls for strong government of a kind that shows scant respect for those conventions. That is why conservative theorists like Michael Oakeshott say that only after generations will understanding of the historically deep conventions in which our political sensibilities are embedded show itself in assured and relatively unselfconscious practice.[3]

Nonetheless, admirable though the spirit of the 1950s was as it showed itself in the behaviour of Australians to 'new Australians', the immigrant experience under an emergent, practical, and for the most part theoretically unselfconscious multiculturalism is better than it was then. In hardly any respect, however, is it an immigrant achievement. It represents a transformation and deepening, by an essentially Anglo-Celtic intelligentsia (writers, academics, artists and journalists—yes the 'chattering classes'), of the tolerance I have already praised. Enchanted (sometimes romantically and sentimentally) by Mediterranean liveliness, colour and warmth (and, of course, food) they were for understandable but mistaken reasons alienated from much of Anglo-Celtic Australia in ways that inclined them to denigrate it. Mindful of that alienation, I was surprised and impressed, when I first went to England in 1972, by the affection and respect much of the English intelligentsia showed to ordinary men and women.

When friends in England, where I spend half of each year, ask me what it is about Australia that engages my affection most deeply, I often tell them two stories. The first is about the behaviour of an Australian soldier towards one of the Dunera Boys—German Jewish men who fled to

Britain from Nazi Germany, were arrested as enemy aliens because they were Germans and then shipped on *SS Dunera* to detention camps to Australia. The Dunera Boy who told the story was at the back of the column as it marched to a camp on the fringes of the desert. The Australian soldier guarding him stopped, handed him his rifle, and said, 'Here mate. Hold this while I to go to have a piss.' The Dunera Boy said that he knew then that he was in heaven.

The second story tells of an incident at the funeral of Dinny O'Hearn, a well-known and loved Melburnian. The chapel filled quickly, so latecomers sat on the steps outside. A high-ranking federal minister arrived. It seemed to me that he had no entourage, but I may not have noticed because his arrival was so inconspicuous. I assumed he would go into the church where a place would have been reserved for him. He made no attempt to do so, but sat without fuss on the steps. I was especially struck by the fact that it evidently hadn't occurred to him to do otherwise. The minister was Gareth Evans, who was not famed for his humility.

Both stories reveal egalitarianism inflected in recognisably Australian ways. Its spirit gives the distinctive character to the decency that showed in, amongst other things, the treatment of white immigrants.

Earlier I said that some people worry that multiculturalism will undermine the capacity of immigrants to develop deep affection, perhaps even love, for Australia, though they are dutiful citizens. They worry because they assume that multiculturalism must, by definition, refuse to privilege the Anglo-Celtic inheritance in Australian national culture, treating it as one of many that together should form a multicultural Australian national identity unified by a common citizenship. Such people, I think, read too much multicultural theory and pay too little attention to the reality on the ground.

When I first heard the Dunera Boy's story—told I think by Terry Lane—it delighted me because I recognised in that soldier the men and women I had known as a boy growing up in Central Victoria. When I wrote *Romulus, My Father,* I reflected on the values that shaped the lives of those Anglo-Celtic people, on how those values determined and were in turn determined by the landscape of the area, and on how that landscape nourished and marked indelibly the souls of many who have loved it.

Most of the immigrants found the countryside alien and hostile. Their children usually came to love it, but often in ways that showed their origins. Because I accepted, and made my own, my father's European fatalism, the light and the colours of Central Victoria became for me the light and colours of tragedy. Elsewhere I have tried to explain how my sense of the landscape of Central Victoria affected the entire mood and tone of my book, even perhaps the rhythm of its sentences. Commenting on my work, many people have remarked that they hear in it a distinctive voice. That voice was formed, growing up as I did, in the landscape of central Victoria—with my Romanian father, with his Romanian friend Pantelimon Hora, haunted by my German mother—and with the Anglo-Celtic men and women who farmed it and worked in its towns.

There are many such stories and there will be many more. Each generation of immigrants will change the tone and resonances of the Anglo-Celtic voice that invites them into conversation about what it means to be Australian. That voice may change radically, but never, I hope, to a degree that makes it unrecognisable to, or in ways that would alienate, those whose sense of what it means to be Australian has been nourished by the Anglo-Celtic pioneers. One might therefore call that hope the expression of an assimilationist ideal of multiculturalism. It differs from the policies of the 1950s because it imposes no assimilationist agenda and because—though it neither pretends nor wishes that the Anglo-Celtic voice, however modulated it may become, should be merely one voice amongst others in the cultural conversation—it recognises that genuine conversation must be open to the unforeseeable.

After the Cronulla riots an eminent Australian thinker told me that she was less troubled by the first riot on the beach than by the brutal efficiency of the response to it by parts of the Lebanese community. She appeared to believe that the Lebanese youths involved had learnt to respond as they did because they had participated in the violence that has torn Lebanon apart or because they had watched it, with deep cultural empathy, on television. I do not know whether she was right, but even if she was, I suspect something deeper troubled her. It was not—at least not in the first instance—that she believed that there would be more and more frequent episodes of lawlessness. She feared, I think, that even when immigrants are law-abiding, the conceptions that some of them have of what that means is profoundly out of touch with the spirit that defines Australia's political identity and its civic virtues. Immigrants from countries whose citizens believe that it is sometimes legitimate to assassinate their political opponents may dutifully reject such beliefs when they become Australian citizens, thereby signing up to one of our 'core values'. But those who do this because they realise that it is on the whole better to live in a society where assassination is not a practice are different from people who are born into a political culture that is partly defined by the fact that it is unthinkable that assassination should be a means of settling even serious political disputes. Martin Krygier put the point elegantly in his book *Civil Passions*: 'Who, for example, thought of reaching for his revolver when

Mr Whitlam was sacked in 1975? The answer, of course, is virtually no one at all. What an extraordinary answer that is, in a struggle over the highest political stakes. In many countries, the answer would—equally obviously—have been: everyone who counts.[14] The difference between those two answers does not show itself in citizenship tests and is not a function of anything that can be taught in schools.

Nations and their political and moral cultures are partly defined by what is undiscussable in them. When something is undiscussable in a culture it is treated as having no serious speaking voice in an argument—treated as something that no one should rightly believe she must listen to with an open mind, allowing herself to be persuaded by it if the argument goes a certain way.

Ethnic cleansing, genocide, the public castration of sex offenders, cutting off the hands, and perhaps other limbs, to punish certain kinds of offenders, stoning women to death for adultery—all these and more are undiscussable for Australians, though of course not only for them. Australians do not allow that argument over them genuinely has two sides, just as we do not allow that there are two sides for the proposition that in order to compete with cheap Asian labour we should enslave our black citizens, or for the proposition that Israeli injustices against the Palestinians suggest that Hitler got at least one thing right. These are uncontroversial and dramatic examples. Less dramatic, but I hope as uncontroversial, is the example with which I introduced this part of my discussion. Australians do not think it arguable whether it is sometimes legitimate to assassinate their political opponents in Australia. It's not that they have considered it and rejected it for moral or practical reasons. They have not weighed its merits and demerits. It is simply not an option. What a nation finds undiscussable or unthinkable is not set in stone. It used to be unthinkable that we would justify torturing people, but we discussed it as a means of protecting ourselves in the so-called war against terror and, I am certain, we will discuss it again: Barack Obama has not done anything, and could not do anything, that would put a stop to this discussion.

Less fundamental, but still important, amongst the elements that define the culture of a people and its national identity are the unwritten conventions that govern civic and political behaviour—in countries like Australia the relative (I stress relative) absence of corruption, the acceptance of ministerial responsibility, high standards of truthfulness—the sorts of untheorised practices that, as I remarked earlier, conservative political philosophers like Michael Oakeshott defend against what they take to be a philistine and thoughtless rationalism.

Some of the things that I listed as unthinkable for us are discussed and practised in countries from which we gather immigrants, or if they are not now practised have been within living memory. Many of the conventions I have mentioned are absent or weak in those countries of origin. But none of that is new and, insofar as the conventions I have described have been eroded, Anglo-Celtic politicians are mostly to blame. Think of the political mendacity of successive governments that deepened the cynicism of many Australian voters. Think also of how governments have recklessly undermined unwritten conventions that protect the institutions essential to democracy from corruption and that justify pride in them—conventions about how politicians behave towards the ABC, the High Court, the public service, the armed forces and parliament, for example, including their attitudes to ministerial responsibility.

So far I have described a non-theoretical multiculturalism that emerged in Australia from the 1960s onwards, partly in response to a growing revulsion against racism, in response to the pained realisation of how pervasive racism can be in even fine people whose good intentions were sometimes polluted by it. The kind of multiculturalism that emerged was also a response to the growing awareness of the wrongs inflicted by colonial regimes on their subject peoples and to a shamed and somewhat frightened realisation of to what extent we, the beneficiaries of colonial exploitation, now suffer the understandable resentments our colonial ancestors provoked. Colonial policy was devised and administered by many kinds of people with intentions and motives they often only partially understood. Full understanding of such things takes time to emerge in the consciousness of a nation because it usually takes time for the members of a generation to acknowledge, in their hearts, that they and the many good people they knew expressed attitudes or were caught up in practices that a clear moral light would reveal to be indefensible. It's a small thing, perhaps, but when I recall the Tarzan films and comics I enjoyed as a boy, I am now astonished by the complacent racism that betrayed itself in the fact that I and others found nothing objectionable in the contempt for black Africans that they often expressed.

More seriously, some of Australia's most influential political pundits have said that commonsense and realism persuaded many 'ordinary Australians' that we must sometimes be prepared to kill thousands of civilians in order to secure America's protection in as yet unforeseen circumstances. That, many pundits say, is why John Howard escaped serious criticism, although no weapons of mass destruction were found in Iraq, and no one believes we invaded Iraq to liberate Iraqis from Saddam's tyranny. We must hope the pundits are wrong. If they are not, it will be very hard for Muslim leaders to convince young radicals in their community that 'ordinary Australians' do not hold Iraqi lives cheap—so cheap that neither we nor our partners in the Coalition of the Willing bothered to count how many we killed. Whenever we preach Australian values this must surely come to the minds of potential suicide bombers and their sympathisers. The difference between killing civilians intentionally and killing them unintentionally—when the latter is, as the disgusting euphemism puts it, 'collateral damage'—is, of course, important. But the full significance of that difference depends on how seriously one does whatever one can to avoid killing them. Amongst other ways, that will show in why one goes to war and the attitude one takes to those who have taken us to war.

It may already be clear why I have said nothing directly about the effect that global terrorism should have on our thoughts about multiculturalism in Australia. I think it should have no effect. That is not because fear of terrorism has diminished in the last few years. It is because most migrants have no connection to terrorism and that will not change when, as is likely, we again have reason to fear terrorist attacks.

If people fear any migrant groups it is those from the Middle East, especially if they are also Muslims. Suppose then, for the sake of argument, that commentators who talk of the clash of civilisations between Western secular democracies and a fanatically politicised Islam are right to warn that Muslims are a threat to the peaceful multicultural mix of Australia and other nations. If true, that would be a problem, of course, but it would discredit multiculturalism only for someone who unjustifiably assumes that it should never require a judgment about which cultures are suitable for the multicultural mix of a particular nation at a particular time. Like all judgments such judgments are fallible. Even if it were true, therefore, that for the foreseeable future Muslim communities would constitute an unstable and dangerous element in an otherwise successful mixture of cultures, why should that panic us into renouncing that successful mixture? Defenders of multiculturalism should not deny that some cultures—or, more often, the historical form of some cultures—might be alien to the multicultural mix that works in a particular country. More strongly, they should admit that just as most cultures are food for the soul, some—or significant parts of them—are poison for it. Imagine Europe fifty years after a Nazi victory.

In Australia we have no reason to think anything like this. No one responsible has suggested that the majority of Muslims are of any concern. They have, after all, been here a long time. Even if they are inclined—as are orthodox Jews—to religious separatism, that need not of itself be a problem for the assimilationist multiculturalism that I have been celebrating. There have been many complaints that Jewish political groups lobby on behalf of Israel even when to do so is against Australian or American interests. But in that respect they are not much different, I suspect, from the National Farmers Federation. True if the farmers compromise Australia's more general interests, they do not do it for the sake of a foreign government. That difference, however, matters only if there is reason to think the behaviour of the Jewish lobbies sometimes constitutes disloyalty to Australia of a kind that would rightly give loyal Australians reasons to be suspicious of the Jewish community. There is no reason whatsoever to believe that. The same is true for the Muslims. And if either community, or any other like community, exceeds the bounds of legitimate lobbying, there are easy remedies for it.

If I am right about the facts, then we in Australia have reason to fear only the murderous ambitions of a handful of radical Muslims driven by a religion based totalitarian politics. They are a problem for the police, the security services, the immigration authorities and other institutions that can identify them and to the extent that it is possible—and it will not always be possible—thwart their murderous intentions. But why do a small number of radical Muslims discredit multiculturalism?

Until now I have defended a kind of multiculturalism against criticism by the right. I want now to turn again to a claim, advanced mostly by the left, that a state for all its citizens, equally 'owned' by each of them and home to a plurality of cultures but whose identity no one of them forms, is our best hope against the evils of nationalism.

It is just a fact of human life that many—perhaps most—people develop deep attachments to places and to institutions. Not all, it is true, and some people have argued that the desire for such attachments expresses an infantile aspect of our nature that hinders the realisation of much of what is distinctive and fine in our humanity. Trees, George Steiner remarked, have roots whereas human beings have legs. Most people, however, don't like to wander all their lives, especially not at the beginning of their lives or at the end. And those who do wander usually rejoice in the diversity of cultures that were first made possible and then made deep by people who planted their roots. Most of the cultures in a multicultural society are national cultures—Italian, Greek, Chinese and so on—whose vitality, whose capacity to resist degenerating into pathetic expressions of nostalgia, depends on the degree to which their members have a creative relation to the nations from which they emigrated.

The soul needs warmth which for most people comes from being in familiar surroundings for which they have affection. Most people's deepest attachments are local—to a particular part of a country, perhaps a farm or a town, sometimes a city. Often it requires something unusual for them to realise that their attachments are wider: to the state (in the sense in which Victoria, for example, is a state) and also, more often than not, to the nation. They may realise that their attachments are more extensive than to their local town only when they are abroad and discover just how pleased they are, if they are Australian, to hear an Australian accent. That is not superficial: poets sometimes dry up in exile. For many people, less fortunate than Australians, the realisation might come when they have lost their country and live under foreign occupation, are denied the right to speak their language, to honour their national institutions, to remember their past fully and to pass on its treasure to future generations. In such terrible circumstances people realise that responsible love of country will seek protection for what is loved and is owed to future generations. In modern times, the means of protection is almost always the nation-state, for it alone has the necessary military power (commonly in alliance with other nation-states). Protection is sought not just for the institutions of citizenship—the rule of law, democracy and so on, as these might be relatively interchangeable between different countries—but for those institutions that are infused by the spirit of a particular people, by their history, their language, their art, their poetry, their song.

Attachments of this kind to place, and the institutions that partly define it and are defined by it, can be identity forming. I don't intend anything seriously theoretical by the expression 'identity forming'. Part of what I mean is shown in a distinctive use of the first-person plural. People have a sense of belonging to a group (to a family, church, neighbourhood, town, nation and so on) when they can identify with that group in ways that enable them to say that *we* did this or that, even though they may not have even taken part in the events to which they refer. In some of my writings, especially those concerned with the idea of collective responsibility, I have called the use of that *we* 'an expression of fellowship', distinguishing it from a *we* that merely records that one belongs to a particular group. It goes with pleasure, sometimes pride, in the achievements of the group, though, once again, one may have done nothing about which one could justifiably feel pride. While it is obvious that these ways of saying *we* have expressed contemptuous and even murderous hostility towards those who are not *we*, who are not 'one of us', but who are 'them', it is equally obvious that this need not be so and often has not been so.

A young Australian might, therefore, say with pride, 'We fought at Gallipoli and in World War II against an evil tyranny,' though she was not even born at the time. If she does so, however, then, appealing to that same sense of collective agency, she should also be prepared to say with then Prime Minister Paul Keating, 'We took the traditional lands, committed the murders, took the children.' If one believes that one can justifiably feel pride in the achievements of one's political ancestors, then one must also be prepared to feel shame for their crimes. To wish to feel proud without accepting the need sometimes to feel shame is to fall victim to that false love of country that we call jingoism. If a sense of national belonging is to be clear-sighted, therefore, it must be constrained, and in submission to that constraint be deepened by the requirements of justice insofar as they are inseparable from a sense of common humanity with all the peoples of the earth.

The point goes deeper than one about consistency. Though the values that determine the difference between patriotism and jingoism have varied historically and culturally, it is essential to the very nature of love of country, as it is to any other form of love, that we mark the difference between its real and counterfeit forms. We would not call something love (be it love of country, romantic love, or parental love, for example) if it were not so answerable, just as we would not call something courage unless it were answerable to the distinction between real courage and recklessness, for example, or grief unless it were answerable to the difference between authentic grief and sentimental self-indulgence. The values expressed in those standards are not imposed from outside but are constitutive of the kind of love in question. Those values that condemn jingoism as a corruption of love of country rather than just another form of it are, as I have suggested, often moral values. But it is controversial whether the moral values that are intrinsic to love of country should, for someone whose love is clear-sightedly informed by an understanding of the place of morality in politics, override other values, distinctive to the political realm, that may be in conflict with them.

Ever since the time of Socrates, Western political thought has been haunted by the belief—or fear—that morality and politics may be in deep and irreconcilable conflict, not because politics is too disreputable for a morally good person to take part in, but because at critical points moral and political conduct belong to incommensurable realms of value, both of which will claim the allegiance of any serious person. That does not mean, of course, that morality and politics are not in deep ways answerable to one another. Morality cannot ignore the claims of politics or politics those of morality. Indeed, for almost everyone who has taken the conflict seriously, the mutual answerability of morality and politics to one another generates tragedy. But that, as I acknowledged earlier, is controversial. Whichever side one takes in this argument, however, one should not think that real love of country belongs to that side alone.

Responding to a letter by Gershom Scholem in which he said that her book *Eichmann in Jerusalem*, and her response to its (often vicious) critics, betrayed that she had no love for the Jewish people, Hannah Arendt replied that she believed that only individual human beings are the proper objects of love.[5] The distinction between love and its many false semblances is fundamental to the concept of love itself, and sometimes the distinction must be invoked in disputes about what kinds of things are the appropriate objects of love. Disputes of that kind cannot be settled by insisting that anything that a person sincerely declares she loves is love's fitting object. Probably of all the passions, love suffers the most plausible impostors. Nor, I think, can such disputes be settled by abstract theories about the nature of love. Thought about love is inescapably informed by and answerable to examples that speak authoritatively while inviting one's critical assessment.

As is often the case with values that go deep, we learn from examples that we trust. We may come to see depth or even sense where we had not seen it before because we are moved by someone's example, by what they do or say or by what they are, in ways that, upon critical reflection, strike us as authoritative. As one would expect of a love that fastens on something that is inevitably a mixture of good and evil, love of country is always a mixture of gratitude, pain, joy, sorrow, pride and shame. When John

Howard declared that he always supported reconciliation, and said that his love for Australia made it impossible for him to apologise for past wrongs suffered by the Aborigines and impossible for him to feel shame for those wrongs, he expressed an interesting and, I suspect, common confusion that corrupts love of country. He spoke as though he believed that an assessment of the balance between the good and evil in our history should make one either proud or ashamed, as though one could not be both, as though the object of pride or shame was always the country, indivisibly, as it were. The country, indivisibly, is the object of love, but pride and shame are for this or that aspect of its history.

We will not avoid aggressive nationalism unless we see, at the very least, that there should be no conflict between our understanding of the common good and the national interest, and our nation's answerability to significant parts of international law—those especially that have to do with the laws of war and with the crimes identified under the concept 'a crime against humanity'. National interest has to do with what is of fundamental importance to people in their role as citizens and patriots. Patriots should therefore acknowledge that real love of country is distinguished from aggressive nationalism by at least two things: it desires to be truthful and it desires to love without the shame that would be the only truthful response if the nation's leaders and soldiers committed crimes that would justifiably bring them before an international criminal court.

There is a reply, therefore, to people who say, for example, that for the sake of the common good and the national interest we should torture terrorists whom we believe have information that might save thousands of lives. It is a reply that appeals to a deeper conception of the common good and the national interest. It says that it is part of a morally enriched idea of the national interest and the common good that we not even consider such things, that we remain a nation whose integrity is partly defined by the fact that such things are unthinkable for it. Of course people will argue about this and, as I said earlier, Obama's presidency will not take discussion of torture off the agenda. My point, however, is that those who argue that torture is sometimes justified because it is necessary to save perhaps thousands of lives cannot appeal to a morally neutral conception of the common good or of the national interest to justify the alleged 'necessity'.

So though I understand the fear people express when they deny that there is a political value deeper than citizenship, I do not believe it is a reason to deny that there can be such a thing as love of country and that it can be lucid and fine. Even when citizenship is inflected in ways I described earlier, it can be cold unless nourished by love of country. Love of country is different from the duties and rights that define citizenship and deeper than the gratitude and pride that citizenship can inspire—deeper because love is deeper than pride, and deeper too than gratitude when gratitude is not itself transformed by love. The understandable fears that talk of love of country arouse in many people are reasons for thinking hard—in ways we seldom do—about how to block the many routes love finds to jingoism and to open the routes by which jingoism can find its way to love. Simone argued in her wonderful book *The Need for Roots* that compassionate love of what is good and fragile rather than only grand, noble and heroic, and lucid humbled acknowledgment of the wrongs we have committed or become caught up in are prerequisites for both.[6] They are also prerequisites if we are justifiably to hope that young immigrants who have been radicalised by a vivid sense of the past evils of colonialism and racism might move beyond mere law-abiding citizenship to affection—perhaps even love—for this country.

For that reason, those who wish to be citizens of the world, who rightly say that we share a common humanity with all the people of the earth, should insist that all nations be fully subject to international law. Our intention should be to make people in the developed Western nations understand, fully in their hearts, that their leaders and their soldiers may be liable to prosecution in an international criminal court. At present we seem to assume that such a fate is suitable only for darker skinned people, for Rwandans, or Chileans or Slavs—wogs of one kind or another. For reasons that have nothing to do with their beliefs about the justice of the invasion of Iraq, most Australians find barely intelligible the suggestion that Howard or Blair or Bush might justifiably face criminal charges for their roles in the invasion.

Simone Weil described being rooted in a national culture as 'food for the soul', and a country as a 'vital medium'.[7] The intentional destruction of anything that gives necessary food for the soul is a crime. Sometimes the crime is genocide, now acknowledged universally to be particularly grave. In her interesting account of why genocide should be called a crime against humanity, Hannah Arendt said genocide is 'an attack upon human diversity as such, upon a characteristic of the human status, without which the very words "mankind" or "humanity" would be devoid of meaning'.[8] In their failure, so radical in its nature, to acknowledge a common humanity with their victims, in their arrogant assumption that they are entitled to decide which peoples are fit to inhabit the earth, the perpetrators of genocide offend against their victims, as individuals and as members of the target group. But their crime is also against the constituency of humankind. The concept of a crime against humanity expresses the belief that those who commit this crime offend against the moral constitution of humanity itself—considered not as a constituency of moral agents, nor of human beings, but of human beings as citizens in the plurality of nations that comprise the community of nations.

Arendt's discussion is important because it shows us, I believe, how to render consistent things that are often thought to be necessarily in conflict with one another. When we call genocide a crime against humanity, we acknowledge our need for roots, for local identity, and also that the ways we protect that need must be answerable to the constituency of humankind as it is represented in the international law of the community of nations. For those who accept Arendt's claim that the plurality of peoples and cultures is fundamental to our very concept of humanity the point is even stronger. For them, respect for the diversity of cultures, peoples and the nations which protect them will be a requirement that is inseparable from the very concept of humanity to which we appeal when we say that actions in defence of those nations must be answerable to the universal principles of justice.

INTRODUCTION

1 John Hirst, *Sense and Nonsense in Australian History*, Black Inc, Melbourne, 2009.

2 http://www.multiculturalaustralia.edu.au/doc/howard_2.pdf

3 In a speech in Washington in 2010, Howard drew the distinction explicitly, praising ethnic and religious tolerance while condemning multiculturalism. 'The Margaret Thatcher Freedom Lecture', 24 September 2010, the Heritage Foundation, Washington, http://www.heritage.org/Events/2010/09/John-Howard
For a transcript: http://www.heritage.org/Research/Lecture/2011/01/The-Anglosphere-and-the-Advance-of-Freedom

4 Peter Costello, 'Worth Promoting, Worth Defending: Australian Citizenship, what it means and how to nurture it', Address to the Sydney Institute, 23 February 2006, http://www.treasurer.gov.au/DisplayDocs.aspx?pageID=&doc=speeches/2006/004.htm&min=phc. (My italics.)

5 ibid.

6 ibid.

7 ibid.

8 Martin Krygier, *Between Fear and Hope: Hybrid Thoughts on Public Values*, Boyer Lectures, ABC Books, Sydney, 1997, for example.

9 David Grossman, 'Terror's Long Shadow', *Guardian*, 21 September, 2001, http://www.guardian.co.uk/world/2001/sep/21/afghanistan.writersreflectionsonseptember11

10 http://www.guardian.co.uk/commentisfree/henryporter

11 Philip Ruddock, 'No Better Friend', American Australian Association, New York, 26 July 2005, www.nswccl.org.au/docs/pdf/Ruddock%20speech20050726.pdf

12 'PM's lack of empathy', *Age*, 17 August 2004, http://www.theage.com.au/articles/2004/08/16/1092508365006.html

MULTICULTURALISM AND TERROR

1 Patricia Karvelas, 'Multiculturalism departs stage left from job's title', *Australian*, 15 September 2010. There are indications, however, that the Gillard government may retain 'multiculturalism' at the policy level. See Kate Lundy, 'Multicultural war of words serves nobody', *Australian*, 6 December 2010.

2 Terry Lane, 'Assimilation is a beaut idea that works', *Age*, 17 July 2005.

3 'Militant longed for suicide mission', *Weekend Australian*, 23–24 July 2005.

4 Bruce Bawer, *While Europe Slept: How Radical Islam Is Destroying the West from Within*, Doubleday, New York, 2006; Melanie Phillips, *Londonistan*, Encounter Books, New York, 2006.
5 Janet Albrechtsen, 'With confident, traditional values comes strength', *Australian*, 21 June 2006.
6 Samuel P. Huntington, *The Clash of Civilizations and the Remaking of World Order*, Simon and Schuster, New York, 1996.
7 John Stone, 'The case for assimilation', *Australian*, 15 August 2005.
8 I develop these points in 'Secularism and Religion in a Multicultural Age', in *Secularism, Religion and Multicultural Citizenship*, ed. G.B. Levey and T. Modood, Cambridge University Press, Cambridge, 2008.
9 Bhikhu Parekh, 'Europe, Liberalism and the "Muslim Question"', in T. Modood, A. Triandafyllidou, and R. Zapata-Barrero (eds.) *Multiculturalism, Muslims and Citizenship: A European Approach*, Routledge, London, 2005, pp. 184–5.
10 Amartya Sen, *Identity and Violence: The Illusion of Destiny*, Penguin, Allen Lane, London, 2006.
11 Keith Windschuttle, 'It's not a race war, it's a clash of cultures', *Australian*, 16 December 2005.
12 For elaboration, see Geoffrey Brahm Levey, 'Multicultural Political Thought in Australian Perspective', in G.B. Levey (ed.) *Political Theory and Australian Multiculturalism*, Berghahn Books, New York, 2008.
13 'Our values or go home: Costello', *Age*, 24 February 2006.
14 Nathan Glazer and Daniel Patrick Moynihan, *Beyond the Melting Pot*, MIT Press, Cambridge, Mass., 1964, p. 290.
15 I consider the French approach to cultural diversity in Geoffrey Brahm Levey, 'What Is Living and What Is Dead in Multiculturalism', *Ethnicities*, vol 9: 1, 2009, pp. 75–93.
16 'New recruit's headpiece sets her apart', *Australian*, 27 November 2004.
17 George Washington, 'A Reply to the Hebrew Congregation of Newport, (c. August 17, 1790)', in P. Mendes-Flohr and J. Reinharz, (eds.), *The Jew in the Modern World: A Documentary History*, second edition, Oxford University Press, 1995.
18 Keith Windschuttle, 'It's not a race war, it's a clash of cultures', *Australian*, 16 December 2005.
19 Bob Birrell and Ernest Healy, 'Out-Marriage and the Survival of Ethnic Communities in Australia', *People and Place*, vol 8: 3, 2000, pp. 37–46.
20 See, respectively, Count Molé, 'Napoleon's Instructions to the

Assembly of Jewish Notables (July 29, 1806)', and The Assembly of Jewish Notables, 'Answers to Napoleon (1806)', in P. Mendes-Flohr and J. Reinharz (eds.), *The Jew in the Modern World: A Documentary History*, second edition, Oxford University Press, 1995. In recent decades, the Jewish intermarriage rate has climbed to over 50 per cent in the USA, however the organised Jewish community continues to view this development with alarm and as something to be combatted.

21 John Goldlust, 'Jews in Australia—A Demographic Profile', in G.B. Levey and P. Mendes (eds.) *Jews and Australian Politics*, Sussex Academic Press, Brighton, 2004, pp. 23–4.

22 'Ruddock's call to behave angers Muslims on holy day', *Australian*, 11 January 2006.

23 Michael Walzer, 'The Last Page', *Dissent*, Fall, 2005.

24 See, for example, John Hirst, 'Aborigines and Migrants: Diversity and Unity in Multicultural Australia', *Australian Book Review*, No. 228, 2001, pp. 30–35; and Keith Windschuttle, *The White Australia Policy*, Macleay Press, Sydney, 2004.

25 See, for example: Stephen Castles, Mary Kalantzis, Bill Cope, and Michael Morrissey, *Mistaken Identity: Multiculturalism and the Demise of Nationalism in Australia*, third edition, Pluto Press, Sydney, 1992; and Donald Horne, *The Avenue of the Fair Go: A Group Tour of Australian Political Thought*, Harper Collins, Sydney, 1997.

26 For an extended discussion of the liberal nationalist model in the Australian context, see Geoffrey Brahm Levey, 'Multiculturalism and Australian National Identity', in G.B. Levey (ed.) *Political Theory and Australian Multiculturalism*, Berghahn Books, New York, 2008.

27 Office of Multicultural Affairs, *National Agenda for a Multicultural Australia*, AGPS, Canberra, 1989, pp. 50–52.

MONOCULTURALISM, MUSLIMS AND MYTH MAKING

1 At the time of writing, the NatWest cricket advertisements could be viewed on YouTube www.youtube.com Search for 'NatWest piggy bank'.

2 '"Offensive" piggy banks on display get the chop', *Lancashire Evening Telegraph*, 21 October 2005, p. 6.

3 *Daily Express*, 24 October 2005, p. 1.

4 'PC piggy or hogwash?', *Media Watch*, ABC Television.

5 'Piggy banks for the chop', *Daily Telegraph*, 25 October 2005, p. 13.

6 'Ron' on Radio 6PR, Perth, 28 October 2005, cited in *Media Watch*, 31 October 2005.

7 *Lancashire Evening Telegraph*, 21 October 2005, p. 6.
8 Email to *Media Watch*, http://www.abc.net.au/mediawatch/img/2005/ep35/natwest.pdf
9 Email to *Media Watch*, http://www.abc.net.au/mediawatch/img/2005/ep35/halifax.pdf
10 Peter Oborne, 'The shameful Islamophobia at the heart of Britain's press', *Independent*, 7 July 2008, Media Weekly.
11 For a fuller (but by no means comprehensive) discussion, see Peter Oborne and James Jones, *Muslims under siege: alienating vulnerable communities*, Democratic Audit, Human Rights Centre, University of Essex, July 2008, pp. 19–23; Ken Livingstone (ed.), *The search for common ground: Muslims, non-Muslims and the UK media*, Greater London Authority, November 2007, pp. 31–50.
12 Kerry Moore, Paul Mason and Justin Lewis, *Images of Islam in the UK: The Representation of British Muslims in the National Print News Media 2000-2008*, Cardiff School of Journalism, Media and Cultural Studies, 7 July 2008, pp. 11–12, http://www.cardiff.ac.uk/jomec/resources/08channel4-dispatches.pdf
The former category represented 32 per cent of all reports analysed, while the latter category accounted for 27 per cent.
13 Stanley Cohen, *Folk Devils and Moral Panics: The Creation of Mods and Rockers*, Basil Blackwell, Oxford, 1972, p. 1.
14 Sean P. Hier, 'Conceptualizing Moral Panic through a Moral Economy of Harm', *Critical Sociology*, 2002, vol 28: 3, pp. 311–334.
15 'Muslim cabbies refuse to carry booze', *Australian*, 2 October 2006, p. 1.
16 'Culture clash', *Star-Tribune*, 25 March 2007, p. 1.
17 'PM condemns shooting', *Herald Sun*, 2 October 2006, p. 13.
18 'Taxi rank offence', *Australian*, 2 October 2006, p. 9.
19 'The veiled conceit of multiculturalism', *Australian*, 24 October 2006, p. 13.
20 Sean P. Hier, p. 313.
21 Zygmunt Bauman, 'The Great War of Recognition', *Theory, Culture & Society*, 2001, vol 18: 2–3, pp. 137–150, 143–146.
22 See for example: Johann Hari, 'Multiculturalism is not the best way to welcome people to our country', *Independent*, 5 August 2005, p. 35; Johann Hari, 'Rowan Williams has shown us one thing—why multiculturalism must be abandoned', *Independent*, 11 February 2006, Comment.
23 Melanie Phillips, *Londonistan*, Encounter Books, New York, 2006.
24 ibid, pp. 57–76.

25 ibid, p. 58.
26 ibid, p. 76.
27 ibid, p. 60.
28 ibid, p. 60.
29 ibid, p. xxiii.
30 Interview with Jerry Falwell, *The 700 Club*, Christian Broadcasting Network, 13 September 2001.
31 Melanie Phillips, p. 69.
32 ibid, p. 60.
33 'Lessons in tolerance', *Independent*, 1 February 2007, pp. 6-7.
34 'Jewish school is cleared in race bias case', *The Times*, 4 July 2008, p. 25.
35 Melanie Phillips, p. 69.
36 'PM hits at "jihad" Muslims', *Australian*, 20 February 2006, p. 2.
37 'Andrews to lead drive for citizens', *Sydney Morning Herald*, 24 January 2007, p. 6.
38 'Citizenship test marks first day with 25 passes', *Australian*, 2 October 2007, p. 8.
39 'PM tells Muslims to learn English', *Australian*, 1 September 2006, p. 1.
40 Michael Bachelard, 'Believers a world apart', *Age*, 23 September 2006, p. 5.
41 'Sect covered up assaults on girls', *Sydney Morning Herald*, 30 December 2006, p. 1.
42 Denis Gregory, 'Sect in a world of its own', *Sydney Morning Herald*, 1988, p. 7.
43 'Brethren mother flouts order', *Age*, 25 June 2007, p. 6.
44 'PM denies role in Brethren donations', *Age*, 23 August 2007, p. 12.
45 Adele Horin, 'Must double standards be met, too?', *Sydney Morning Herald*, 30 September 2006, p. 33.
46 'English take-up speaks volumes for Muslims', *Sydney Morning Herald*, 18 November 2006, p. 7.
47 Melanie Phillips, p. xxi.
48 ibid, p. xx.
49 *Dispatches: It shouldn't happen to a Muslim*, Channel 4, 7 July 2008. (Emphasis added.)
50 Geoffrey Brahm Levey, 'The antidote of multiculturalism', *Griffith Review* 15, 2007, pp. 197–208, 201.
51 Janet Albrechtsen, 'Multicultural madness needs such antidotes', *Australian*, 18 October 2006, p. 12.
52 See for example: Janet Albrechtsen, 'Open market on democratic

ideals', *Australian*, 3 May 2006, p. 12.

53 Melanie Phillips, p. xx.

54 ibid, pp. 73–74.

55 ibid, p. xviii. There is, however, compelling evidence of the opposite: John L. Esposito and Dalia Mogahed, *Who Speaks for Islam?: What a billion Muslims really think*, Gallup Press, New York, 2007, pp. 65–98.

56 Melanie Phillips, p. xix.

57 The *Beth Din* is part of the United Synagogue, which was established by the *Jewish United Synagogues Act* 1870 (UK). Its decisions may be legally binding under British law as a form of arbitration.

58 'Jewish student's exam shifted after legal threat', *The Times Higher Education Supplement*, 29 May 2008, p. 14.

59 I have discussed more fully elsewhere how meanings—including politicised ones—are projected onto veiling that are neither grounded in Islamic doctrine, nor necessarily shared by the women who wear veils themselves: Waleed Aly, *People Like Us: how arrogance is dividing Islam and the West*, Picador, Sydney, 2007, pp. 104–25.

60 'Girl says top spin bowler shows why she must wear Sikh bangle', *The Times*, 18 June 2008, p. 5.

61 Melanie Phillips, p. 69.

62 ibid, p. 58.

63 Kerry Moore, Paul Mason and Justin Lewis, pp. 10–11. (Emphasis in original.)

64 Ken Livingstone, p. 23.

65 The study found that 80 per cent of articles in the *Independent* and 85 per cent in the *Guardian* were 'negative': ibid.

66 Peter Oborne and James Jones, p. 15.

67 ibid, p. 16.

68 ibid, pp. 14, 16. The article in question is cited as 'In defence of Islamophobia', *Independent*, 23 October 1997.

69 'We must be free to criticise without being called racist', *Guardian*, 18 August 2004, p. 18.

70 'Children of 15 groomed to carry out terrorist acts, MI5 head says', *The Times*, 6 November 2007, p. 6.

71 Domonic A. Bearfield, 'The Demonization of Patronage: Folk Devils, Moral Panics and the *Boston Globe's* Coverage of the Terrorist Attacks of 9/11', *International Journal of Public Administration*, 2008, vol 31: 5, pp. 515–534, 517.

72 Peter Oborne, 'Is Britain Anti-Muslim?', *Daily Mail,* 4 July 2008, pp. 36–7.

73 'UK majority back multiculturalism', *BBC News (Online)*, 10 August 2005, http://news.bbc.co.uk/2/hi/uk_news/4137990.stm
74 'Howard got it wrong on racism: poll', *Age*, 20 December 2005, p. 1.
75 Peter Oborne and James Jones, pp. 12–13.
76 See generally Norman Daniel, *Islam and the West: The making of an image*, Edinburgh University Press, 1960.
77 Melanie Phillips, pp. 19–35.
78 'Taxi rank offence', *Australian*, 2 October 2006, p. 9.
79 James Button, 'Europe divided over response to calls of Islam', *Sydney Morning Herald*, 12 March 2007, p. 12.
80 Interview with Chris Smith, *Radio 2GB*, 31 August 2006.
81 See generally Meyda Yegenoglu, *Colonial Fantasies: Towards a feminist reading of Orientalism*, Cambridge University Press, 1998.
82 'Man of two halves snubs beautiful game', *The Times*, 11 October 2007, p. 37.
83 Melanie Phillips, p. 58.
84 ibid, p. 59.
85 ibid, p. xx.
86 ibid, p. 59.
87 Commonwealth of Australia, *Becoming an Australian Citizen*, Department of Immigration and Citizenship, Canberra, 2007, pp. 5, 13.
88 See for example John Howard, 'Towards one destiny', *Australian*, 26 January 2006, p. 14.
89 Mark Silk, 'Notes on the Judeo-Christian Tradition in America', *American Quarterly*, 1984, vol 36: 1, pp. 65–85, 65–66.
90 Menachem Begin, *The Revolt*, W. H. Allen, London, 1979, p. 28.
91 See generally Arthur A. Cohen, *The Myth of the Judeo-Christian Tradition and Other Dissenting Essays*, Schocken Books, New York, 1971.
92 Mark Silk, p. 66.
93 *Daily Express*, 24 October 2005, p. 1.
94 'Taxi rank offence', *Australian*, 2 October 2006, p. 9.
95 Melanie Phillips, p. 59.
96 'We are all better off being British—and proud of it', *Sunday Telegraph*, 9 December 2007, p. 4.
97 For a comprehensive demonstration of this, see the seminal work: Benedict Anderson, *Imagined Communities: Reflections on the origin and spread of nationalism*, Verso, London, 1983.
98 Geoffrey Brahm Levey, p. 207.
99 Commonwealth of Australia, *Becoming an Australian Citizen*,

Department of Immigration and Citizenship, Canberra, 2007, p. 5.
100 Janet Albrechtsen, 'Move over multiculturalism, your time is past', *Australian*, 29 November 2006, p. 16.
101 Catarina Kinnvall, 'Globalization and Religious Nationalism: Self, Identity, and the Search for Ontological Security', *Political Psychology*, 2004, vol 25: 5, pp. 741–67, 762.
102 ibid, p. 758.
103 ibid, p. 749.
104 ibid, p. 755.
105 I have done this in some detail in Waleed Aly, *People Like Us: How arrogance is dividing Islam and the West*, Picador, Sydney, 2007, pp. 248–261.

ON BEING MUSLIM AND AUSTRALIAN

1 Hansard, 10 September 1996, http://parlinfo.aph.gov.au/parlInfo/search/display/display.w3p;query=Id%3A%22chamber%2Fhansardr%2F1996-09-10%2F0048%22
2 'Hanson "sick of Muslims"', *Age*, 16 August 2007, http://www.theage.com.au/news/national/hanson-sick-of-muslims/2007/08/16/1186857636317.html
3 Radio interview, 13 September 2001, 3AK, Peter Reith interviewed by Derryn Hinch.
4 Daniel Pipes, 'Sudden Jihad Syndrome', Frontpage.com, 14 March 2006, http://frontpagemag.com/Articles/Read.aspx?ARTID=5225
5 John Stone, 'A bigger storm is brewing', *Australian,* 17 November 2006.
6 Alan Jones, 30 July 2001, cited in *Media Watch*, 9 September 2002. Miranda Devine, *Sun Herald*, 12 August 2001, cited in *Media Watch*, 9 September 2002.
7 'Muslim leader blames women for sex attacks', *Australian*, 26 October 2006.

TESTING TIMES

1 *Guardian*, 2 May 2007.
2 Compare Bhikhu Parekh, *A New Politics of Identity: Political Principles for an Interdependent World*, Palgrave Macmillan, London, 2008, p. 287.
3 *Hansard*, House of Representatives, 30 May 2007, p. 7.
4 *Age*, 1 August 2007.
5 *Senate Legal and Constitutional Affairs Committee Inquiry into the Australian Citizenship Amendment (Citizenship Testing) Bill, 2007*,

http://www.aph.gov.au/Senate/committee/legcon_ctte/completed_inquiries/2004-07/citizenship_testing/submissions/sublist.htm

6 *Age*, 29, 30 January 2008. An analysis of the test results appeared in *Australian Citizenship Test: Snapshot Report*, April 2008, http://www.citizenship.gov.au/_pdf/citztest-snapshot-report-2008-april.pdf

7 *Sydney Morning Herald*, 29 April 2008.

8 *Moving forward...Improving pathways to citizenship: A report by the Australian Citizenship Test Review Committee*, August 2008, p. 2. (the phrase 'under God' is discretionary). http://www.citizenship.gov.au/_pdf/moving-forward-report.pdf

9 *Moving forward*, pp. 23–24.

10 Speech, 27 February 2007, http://www.hm-treasury.gov.uk/newsroom_and_speeches/speeches/chancellorexchequer/speech_chx_270207.cfm

11 14 January 2006, http://www.hm-treasury.gov.uk/newsroom_and_speeches/press/2006/press_03_06.cfm

12 Lord Goldsmith QC, Citizenship Review, *Citizenship: Our Common Bond*, March 2008, http://www.justice.gov.uk/docs/citizenship-report-full.pdf

13 Anthony Field and Jane Roberts, 'British Identity: its sources and possible implications for civic attitudes and behaviour', http://www.justice.gov.uk/docs/british-identity.pdf

14 See for example, Rodney Tiffin and Ross Gittins, *How Australia Compares*, Cambridge University Press, Melbourne, 2004, pp. 238 ff; David Denemark, Gabrielle Meagher, Shaun Wilson, Mark Western and Timothy Phillips (eds.), *Australian Social Attitudes 2: Citizenship, Work and Social Aspirations*, UNSW Press, Sydney, 2007.

15 Peter Mandler, *The English National Character: The History of an Idea from Edmund Burke to Tony Blair*, Yale University Press, New Haven and London, 2006, pp. 225–242.

16 Goldsmith, p. 7.

17 Graeme Davison, *Narrating the Nation in Australia*, the Menzies Lecture 2009, Menzies Centre for Australian Studies, King's College, London, 2010.

18 The most celebrated advocate of this view, Samuel Huntington, *The Clash of Civilizations and the Remaking of the World Order*, Simon and Schuster, New York, 1996, argues that the defence of Western civilisation calls for a revival of the religious traditions on which it is based.

19 David Conway, 'Why History Remains the Best Form of Citizenship Education', *Civitas Review*, vol 2: 2, July 2005,

pp. 1–9. For a contrasting view, defending the teaching of history from citizenship education see Sean Lang, 'History and the Britishness Scare', *Around the Globe*, Monash Institute for the Study of Global Movements, vol 4: 3, Winter 2008, pp. 20–25.

20 For a range of such views see submissions to the Senate Legal and Constitutional Affairs Committee Inquiry into the *Australian Citizenship Amendment (Citizenship Testing) Bill 2007*, http://www.aph.gov.au/Senate/committee/legcon_ctte/completed_inquiries/2004-07/citizenship_testing/submissions/sublist.htm

21 For an excellent exposition of this viewpoint see Parekh, *A New Politics of Identity*, pp. 239–58.

22 The following writers, while differing in important ways about the weight to be given to group identity and national cohesion, agree broadly on such a civic republican conception of citizenship. The Canadian philosopher Charles Taylor, 'Shared and Divergent Values' (1991) in his *Reconciling the Solitudes*, McGill-Queens, Quebec, 1993, and *The Ethics of Authenticity*, Harvard University Press, Cambridge, Mass, 1991, was important in showing how group identity could be reconciled with national citizenship. At the 'multicultural' pole of this debate are writers like Bhikhu Parekh, *Rethinking Multiculturalism: Cultural Diversity and Political Theory*, second edition, Palgrave Macmillan, London, 2006; idem, *A New Politics of Identity*, and Amartya Sen, *Identity and Violence: The Illusion of Destiny*, W.W. Norton, New York, 2006; in a more central position is David Miller, *Citizenship and National Identity*, Polity Press, London, 2000, while David Goodhart, *Progressive Nationalism*, Demos Foundation, London, 2006, emphasises national values and cohesion rather than group identities and rights.

23 David Goodhart, *Progressive Nationalism*, Demos Foundation, London, 2006.

24 On this point, see David Miller, 'Group Identities, National Identities and Democratic Politics' in his *Citizenship and National Identity*, Polity Press, London, 2000, pp. 62–80.

25 Tim Soutphommasane, *Reclaiming Patriotism: Nation Building for Australian Progressives*, Cambridge University Press, Melbourne, 2009, esp. pp. 20–23, 43–45. The study builds on the author's Oxford D.Phil thesis written under the supervision of the political philosopher David Miller, a leading British advocate for a progressive nationalism.

26 See Bernard Crick, *Essays on Citizenship*, and Andrew Lockyer, Bernard Crick and John Annette (eds.), *Education for Citizenship:*

Issues of Theory and Practice, Ashgate, Aldershot, 2003. Crick offered an oblique commentary on the Australian debate in his April 2007 Seymour Lecture at the University of Sydney: 'Citizenship and Democracy: Civic Republicanism or Liberalism?', http://www.seymour.usyd.edu.au/ideas/07past.shtml

27 'History Teaching and Nationalism', *Around the Globe*, vol 4: 3, Winter 2008, pp. 14–19; Anna Clark, *History's Children: History Wars in the Classroom*, UNSW Press, 2008. For broader arguments along these lines see John Tosh, *Why History Matters*, Palgrave Macmillan, London, 2008, pp. 120–39 and Graeme Davison, *The Use and Abuse of Australian History*, Allen & Unwin, Sydney, 2000, pp. 178–96, 272–74.

28 *Life in the United Kingdom: A Journey to Citizenship*, third impression, 2007.

29 *Life in Australia*, Australian Government: Department of Immigration and Citizenship, first impression, Canberra, September 2007.

30 Bhikhu Parekh, *Rethinking Multiculturalism: Cultural Diversity and Political Theory*, second edition, Palgrave Macmillan, London, 2006, p. 352.

31 *Australian Citizenship: Our Common Bond*, Australian Government: Department of Immigration and Citizenship, Canberra, 2009, p. 69.

32 *Moving forward*, p. vii.

33 *Moving forward*, p. 22 (my italics).

34 *Reclaiming Patriotism*, p. 42.

35 The following paragraphs are based on comments on the test from prospective applicants at www.australiantest.com/ad

MULTICULTURALISM AND THE UNGOVERNABLE MUSLIM

1 U. Hannerz, *Transnational Connections: Culture, People, Places*, Routledge, New York, 1996.

2 R. Brague, *The Law of God: the philosophical history of an idea*, trans. L. G. Cochrane, University of Chicago Press, 2007.

3 A. Phoenix and A. Rattansi, 'Rethinking youth identities: modernist and postmodernist frameworks'. *Identity: An International Journal of Theory and Research*, vol 5: 2, 2005, pp. 97–123.

4 G. Hage, *White Nation: fantasies of white supremacy in a multicultural society*, Pluto Press, Sydney, 1998.

5 L. Althusser, *Lenin and Philosophy and Other Essays*, trans. B. Brewster, Monthly Review Press, New York, 1971.

6 D. Moses and G. Brahm Levey, 'The Muslims are our Misfortune!', in G. Noble (ed.), *Lines in the Sand: The Cronulla Riots and the Limits of Australian Multiculturalism*, Institute of Criminology, Sydney, 2009, pp. 98–110.

7 F. Galbally, *Migrant services and programs: report of the Review of Post-arrival Programs and Services for Migrants*, Australian Government Publishing Service, Canberra, 1978.

8 The publishing on 30 September 2005 by the Danish *Jyllands-Posten*, and then by other European newspapers, of cartoons that made fun of the Prophet Muhammad as a way of asserting Europe's valorisation of free speech.

MULTICULTURALISM, LOVE OF COUNTRY AND RESPONSES TO TERRORISM

1 John Hirst, *Sense and Nonsense in Australian History*, Black Inc, Melbourne, 2009.

2 Rowan Williams, 'Civil and Religious Law in England: A Religious Perspective', Foundation Archbishop's Lecture, Royal Courts of Justice, February 2008, http://www.archbishopofcanterbury.org/1575

3 Michael Oakeshott, *Rationalism in Politics and Other Essays*, Methuen, London, 1977.

4 Martin Krygier, *Civil Passions: Selected Essays*, Black Inc, Melbourne, 2005.

5 Hannah Arendt, *The Jew as Pariah: Jewish Identity and Politics in the Modern Age*, Grove Press, New York, 1978, p. 246.

6 Simone Weil, *The Need for Roots: Prelude to a Declaration of Duties Towards Mankind*, Routledge, London, 2001.

7 ibid.

8 Hannah Arendt, *Eichmann in Jerusalem: A Report on the Banality of Evil*, Viking Press, New York, 1964.